GOLD DISCOVERY JOUR
F 865 S66 1990

P9-DVH-962

THE GOLD DISCOVERY JOURNAL
OF AZARIAH SMITH

Azariah Smith, third from left, with other surviving eyewitnesses of the California gold discovery, from left, Henry W. Bigler, William J. Johnston, and James S. Brown, at the 1898 Golden Jubilee in San Francisco. Courtesy of Bigler family.

The Gold Discovery Journal
of Azariah Smith

edited by
David L. Bigler

University of Utah Press
Salt Lake City
1990

Volume Seven, Publications in Mormon Studies
Linda King Newell, editor

Publications in Mormon Studies was established to encourage creation and submission of work on Mormon-related topics that would be of interest to scholars and the general public. The initiation of the series represents an acknowledgment by the Press and the editor of the region's rich historical and literary heritage and of the quality of work being done in various areas of Mormon studies today.

∞ The paper in this book meets the standards for permanence and durability established by the Committee on Production Guidelines for Book Longevity of the Council of Library Resources.

Library of Congress Cataloging-in-Publication Data

Smith, Azariah, d. 1912-
    The gold discovery journal of Azariah Smith / edited by David L. Bigler.
        p.   cm. — (Publications in Mormon studies, ISSN 0893-4916 ; v. 7)
    Includes bibliographical references.
    ISBN 0-87480-346-2 (alk. paper)
    1. California—Description and travel—To 1848. 2. California—Gold discoveries. 3. Smith, Azariah, d. 1912—Diaries.
4. Overland journeys to the Pacific. 5. West (U.S.)—Description and travel—To 1848. 6. Pioneers—California—Diaries. 7. Mormons—California—Diaries.   I. Bigler, David L., 1927- . II. Title.
III. Series.
F865.S66   1990
979.4'03—dc20   89-40597
                                                          CIP

CONTENTS

MAPS AND ILLUSTRATIONS

PREFACE

Azariah Smith of the Mormon Battalion was one of two men, and two only, who took part in the American occupation of California in 1846–47, the discovery of gold at Sutter's Mill in January 1848, and the opening of a new wagon road over the Sierra Nevada to the gold fields six months later, and wrote about what they saw in personal diaries. The other was Henry William Bigler, also a member of the Mormon command.

For more than a century, starting with Hubert Howe Bancroft, historians have recognized the importance of Bigler's accounts of these decisive events in the history of California and the West. The objectivity of the spare Virginian, then in his thirties, places the several versions he prepared from his journals in a class by themselves as source works. Among the latest to base a book on one of these was University of California historian Erwin G. Gudde whose *Bigler's Chronicle of the West* was published in 1962.

A companion of Bigler throughout this period was the slender teenager, Smith, who stood very straight at five feet ten or eleven inches and weighed not more than 130 pounds, usually less. Both served in the battalion's Company B, both worked for James Marshall when gold was found on the American River's South Fork, and both belonged to the party that opened the Mormon-Carson Pass Emigrant Trail, a thoroughfare for the gold rush.

Like his older comrade, Smith for most of his life kept pocket diaries which he later transcribed in ink into two large books with lined pages and covers of cardboard wrapped in percale cloth. He entitled this handwritten record, "A Journal or History of Azariah Smith, his travail &c in the Mormon Battalion, In the Service of the United States, to California; and from there to Salt Lake Valley."

After his death in 1912, the two-volume journal was preserved by his sister, Esther Smith Anderson of Manti, Utah, from whom it passed to Annie Watt Anderson, wife of Esther Anderson's son, William. Annie Anderson kept the records in a trunk at her Sanpete County farm until 1939 when she gave them to her daughter, Hazel Anderson Bigler, my mother, who placed them with the History Department of the Church of Jesus Christ of Latter-day Saints (Mormon) for safekeeping about 1954.

With her assistance, I obtained in 1965 a microfilm copy for the purpose, now fulfilled with mother's encouragement and support, to publish this important historical record. From microfilm, the complete journal has been reproduced by the Xerox process as handwritten pages, now in my possession, available for inspection on request.

Revealed by these writings is the hopeful spirit of a young man who was more sensitive to his surroundings and less given to complain than most of his fellows. They show him often homesick, but always optimistic and filled with wonder at the world around him, where he found pleasure in small things. The pages of his journal also testify to his literacy and gentle nature, both probably acquired from his mother, Esther Dutcher Smith.

In presenting the period from July 1846 through September 1848, I have undertaken to provide a reliable source for historians. Additions, always indicated by brackets, have been made only to render some misspelled words easier to read or to restore probable letters, words, or names lost from breakage, fortunately infrequent, along the edge of pages made brittle by age. Punctuation has been modified to replace semicolons with commas or to end sentences with periods. Proper names have been uniformly capitalized and every sentence made to begin with a capital letter. With these limited exceptions, words and sentences have been reproduced as Smith wrote them at the time without deletions.

At the same time, I have undertaken to enhance the interest of readers whose devotion to western history is less than professional. To place Smith's story within the context of the period and provide background information, his account is offered in five parts, each with a brief introduction and ample footnotes. An interested reader should be able to retrace the young Mormon's travels from Fort Leavenworth to the Pacific Ocean, from San Diego to Sutter's Mill, and from the Sierra Nevada's western foothills to Salt Lake Valley.

In presenting this work, I wish especially to acknowledge with appreciation the kindness and professionalism of Librarian Sibylle

Zemitis and other staff members of the California State Library, California Section, Sacramento, the cooperation of the Utah State Historical Society, and the contribution of historian Harold Schindler of Salt Lake City.

Finally, to the three extraordinary women, Esther Smith Anderson, Annie Watt Anderson, and my mother, Hazel Anderson Bigler, who preserved with loving hands for so many years the journal of Azariah Smith and the role he played in the history of California and the West, this book is dedicated.

INTRODUCTION

The travels of Azariah Smith to the Far West in 1846 began with the dream of an American president who would shape the destiny of his country as few of its leaders have ever done. When he was sworn in at age forty-nine, however, there was little about him to suggest that he would become one of the nation's most important, if least recognized, heads of state.

The eleventh president of the United States was to the core a party man, a "pure, whole-hogged Democrat," in the words of one.[1] In the U.S. House of Representatives, where he had served as speaker, his undeviating loyalty to Andrew Jackson had earned him the nickname, "Young Hickory." Against his own will, but to serve the party, he had resigned his seat in Congress to run for governor of his home state where he was elected once and twice defeated.

The first dark horse ever nominated for the presidency, he had received no votes at all at the contested 1844 Democratic Convention until the eighth ballot. Finally chosen as a compromise candidate pledged to serve one term only, he had gone on to win the election that year by less than a majority of the popular vote.

Lacking the eloquence or charisma of such contemporaries as Henry Clay and Daniel Webster, the new president owed his success to hard work, forthright honesty, and attention to detail. Much about him was told by his approach to the office: "I prefer to supervise the whole operations of the government myself rather than entrust the public business to subordinates and this makes my duties very great."[2]

---

[1] Eugene Irving McCormac, *James K. Polk, A Political Biography* (Berkeley: University of California Press, 1922), 239. Also see Charles G. Sellers, *James K. Polk*, 2 vols. (Princeton: Princeton University Press, 1957, 1966).

[2] Milo Milton Quaife, ed., *The Diary of James K. Polk during His Presidency, 1845 to 1849*, 4 vols. (Chicago: A. C. McClurg & Co., 1910), 4:261.

1

But James Knox Polk of Tennessee saw in his mind an American republic much as it exists today, larger by a million square miles or more than it was at the start of his presidency, with enough new territory to encompass all or part of a dozen future states and more than 1,500 miles of Pacific Ocean front. And he was determined to fulfill this vision in the time allowed him—a single term—just four years.

Before he took office in March 1845, Congress and his predecessor, John Tyler, had already approved an offer to annex Texas. But this hardly began to satisfy the new president who wanted to increase the national domain still further by the addition of New Mexico and the prize he most coveted, California.

Polk would have preferred "in a liberal and friendly spirit"[3] to acquire these largely empty regions from Mexico by purchase and the settlement of American claims. Although a prudent man with the public purse, he was nevertheless prepared to bid all the way up to $40 million for a new boundary along the thirty-second parallel from El Paso to the Pacific, "if it could not be had for less."[4] But he was also ready to take more direct action if the opportunity arose.

Intentionally or not, the president himself forced the issue early in 1846, when he positioned a small American army at the mouth of the Rio Grande on a disputed strip claimed by both Texas and Mexico. At the provocation, Mexican cavalry crossed the river in April and ambushed U.S. dragoons. American blood was shed, the public was outraged, and Polk had the chance he needed. It was like an answer to the Methodist president's prayers.

Consistent with his vision was Polk's strategy in waging the war that followed. He moved to invade and hold New Mexico and California for eventual annexation under the peace settlement. At the same time, he aimed to strike hard at the heart of Mexico and end the war quickly at the lowest possible cost to either side. And he intended to accomplish this before his term of office ran out or the opponents of American expansion could frustrate his purpose.

From the outset, the president worried less about Mexico than he did about Great Britain and what this traditional enemy was up

---

[3] J. Buchanan to W. S. Parrott, March 28, 1845, *The Works of James Buchanan*, quoted in McCormac, *Polk*, 384.

[4] Quaife, *Polk Diary*, 1:33–35.

to on the Pacific Coast. American consuls at Mazatlan and Monterey, apparently for reasons of job enhancement, kept such concern alive at Washington with frequent alarms over British designs to add California to their holdings in the New World.

With one eye on the British, Polk with his advisors was about to decide what forces would be needed to occupy New Mexico and move on to invade California when he received an appeal from one Jesse C. Little who termed himself an "Agent of the Church of Jesus Christ of Latter-day Saints in the Eastern States."[5] It was not the first time the members of this controversial sect, commonly called Mormons, had turned to the federal government for help.

Following the short, but brutal Mormon War of 1838 in Missouri, Joseph Smith, the founding prophet of this American faith, had gone to Washington to seek redress for losses suffered by his followers when they were driven from that state. He received sympathy, but no money, from President Van Buren and Congress.

Just before he was murdered in 1844, Smith had proposed federal legislation empowering him to raise a force of 100,000 volunteers, independent of the U.S. Army, to project American power from Texas to Oregon on the frontier. Apparently linked to plans for a Mormon migration west, the idea of a "private army" won little favor or serious notice in Washington.

But later, amid escalating conflict in western Illinois, Smith's successors had looked to government for the means to move their people out of the United States to a new location in the far west. Most of the faithful were concentrated in the city-state of Nauvoo on the Mississippi River in western Illinois, but there were many converts in other parts of America and in foreign countries as well.

Told by Brigham Young in 1845 to round up believers in the eastern states, "clear yourself and go" to California,[6] Samuel Brannan, a young Mormon newspaper editor at New York, had headed first for Washington to seek government mail contracts to finance the trip.

---

[5] J. C. Little to J. K. Polk, June 1, 1846, reprinted with Little's report in William E. Berrett and Alma Burton, *Readings in L.D.S. Church History*, 2 vols. (Salt Lake City, 1953, 1955), 2:204–13.

[6] B. Young to S. Brannan, September 15, 1845, cited in Journal History (typescript, Historical Department, Church of Jesus Christ of Latter-day Saints, Salt Lake City, Utah, microfilm copy available at Brigham Young University, Provo, Utah).

He won little notice in official circles, but did manage to involve himself in a questionable deal[7] (later repudiated by Young) with a former cabinet officer of the Jackson administration, before sailing off in February 1846, with some 230 Mormons on the ship *Brooklyn*, bound for San Francisco Bay.

Young himself, late in 1845, had requested federal contracts to build a string of stockades and blockhouse forts to protect emigrants on the Oregon Trail. He was told that federal troops would probably build the stations; otherwise, interested contractors would be required to submit bids.

Less than three weeks before the first Mormon companies crossed the frozen river into Iowa, Young and his Council of Twelve Apostles on January 20, 1846, had named Jesse C. Little to take charge of the church's operations in the eastern states and given the thirty-year-old New Englander his instructions. To emphasize the importance of his mission, the letter of appointment was datelined: "Temple of God, Nauvoo."

"If our government shall offer any facilities for emigrating to the western coast," these authorities directed, *"embrace those facilities,* if possible." With time running out, they said: "Be thou a savior and a deliverer."[8]

To meet this injunction, Little had obtained letters of introduction, including one from the governor of his home state, New Hampshire, and made an influential new friend in Thomas L. Kane, son of a leading Philadelphia Democrat, who opened some doors in the Polk administration. But he also became entangled with Amos Kendall (the same political opportunist who had persuaded Brannan to sign away future land claims in California) and seemed to make no more headway in attracting the federal arm than those who had tried before.

After ten fruitless days in Washington, the impulsive emissary was moved on June 1 to pen a direct appeal to the president of the

---

[7] For more on Brannan's contract with Amos G. Kendall, postmaster general in the Jackson administration, see Paul Bailey, *Sam Brannan and the California Mormons* (Los Angeles: Westernlore Press, 1943), 24–26.

[8] B. Young to J. C. Little, January 20, 1846 (typescript, Utah State Historical Society).

United States.[9] His letter produced a surprising response because it delivered, apparently at Kane's suggestion, a carefully worded threat calculated to get Polk's attention, and it went to a chief of state who trusted no one but himself to read the mail.

Little began his petition with an emotional account of how the Mormons had been "whipped and stoned, butchered and murdered" for their religious beliefs. He said his people had been compelled to go into the "howling wilderness" and find a new home in the very place Polk had in mind to take over, California. He told the president that as many as 15,000 Mormons were already on their way there, that thousands more were "making ready to go," and another 40,000 or so from Great Britain were also "determined to gather" at that location. The numbers Little gave, outrageously exaggerated, added up to at least four times the known population of Mexico's northernmost province on the Pacific Ocean, not counting Indians.

Despite the injustices they had suffered, Little went on, the Mormons were "true hearted Americans, true to our country, true to its laws, true to its glorious traditions." They would "disdain to receive assistance from a foreign power," he said, unless their own government "will not help us, but compel us to be foreigners."[10] He might have said British, but the president got the message.

The very day he received this remarkable epistle, Polk concluded a "few hundred of the Mormons" should be allowed to serve with the occupation forces in California and sent word that he wanted to see the author at noon the next day, June 3, in the White House. His purpose in seeing the Mormon agent, Polk confided to his diary, was "to prevent this singular sect from becoming hostile to the

---

[9] In an exchange of letters with Samuel Brannan in 1886, Little said of himself: "It has been the fault of my life to act promptly. It is my nature to think rapidly and act while the thought lingers with me. I am like your Electric Battery. When charged a touch charges me with action. In common life I am like an old shoe. But when aroused I am like a Lion started from his lair & have hardly failed to accomplish my purpose. In 1846 nearly 40 years ago at Washington and in the East I had no counsellors, but acted promptly upon my own judgement." See J. C. Little to S. Brannan, March 16, 1886, Vault Manuscript, MSS 29 through 40, Harold B. Lee Library, Brigham Young University, Provo, Utah.

[10] Little to Polk, June 1, 1846.

U.S.,"[11] but he also wanted to make certain Little's professions of loyalty could be relied on if help was given.

Satisfied after a three-hour meeting, the president authorized the enlistment "on their arrival in that country" of 500 or more Mormons "to conciliate them, and prevent them from assuming a hostile attitude towards the U.S."[12] Just to be on the safe side, however, he limited their number to not more than one-fourth of the American occupation force.

On two subsequent occasions, Little saw the president and pressed for approval to enlist the Mormon volunteers as soon as they could be signed up "so that their pay might commence from that time,"[13] but met a courteous, yet firm refusal. Polk had no wish to alert the Mexicans or his political enemies in Congress that an American commander had been ordered to occupy California, if possible, before the winter of 1846–47 set in. Nor did he want to alarm American settlers on the West Coast with the news that the first U.S. troops to arrive there would be Mormons.

But Polk could not know that his position had already been nullified by orders sent June 3 to Colonel Stephen W. Kearny at Fort Leavenworth which failed to make clear that the Mormons were to be enlisted only after they reached California. The carelessly drafted order from Secretary of War William L. Marcy seemed designed instead to demonstrate why Polk preferred to do everything himself rather than delegate responsibility to subordinates.

Advising that a "large body of Mormon emigrants are *en route* to California," Marcy instructed the officer to enlist "their cooperation in taking possession of, and holding that country." To this end, he was authorized "to muster into service such as can be adduced to volunteer; not, however, to a number exceeding one-third of your entire force."[14] The same orders also approved the enlistment of other American settlers on the West Coast.

Up to then, there had been little difficulty in attracting young men from western Missouri to serve with Kearny's 300 or so dragoon

---

[11] Quaife, *Polk Diary*, 1:446.

[12] Ibid.

[13] Ibid., 449.

[14] W. L. Marcy to S. W. Kearny, June 3, 1846, in Exec. Doc. 60, H. R., 30th Cong., 1st sess., 1847–48, 153–55.

regulars so long as the new volunteers were allowed to go to glory on horseback. But when it came to walking, there was an outright "aversion in that section of the State," as the Missouri governor himself had to admit, "to the foot service."[15] With Marcy's order came the opportunity to add a battalion of infantry to Kearny's little Army of the West, and the future general wasted no time in making the most of it.

On June 19, he ordered Captain James Allen, First Dragoons, to go at once to Mormon emigration camps in Iowa and raise four or five companies of foot soldiers, each numbering from 73 to 109, to serve for twelve months under his command. Once they were mustered, Allen was told to march the recruits back to Fort Leavenworth where they would be "armed and prepared for the field" before following the American invasion force in the "direction of Santa Fe."[16]

To the forty-year-old West Point graduate whose seventeen years of service had seen precious few opportunities for promotion, the assignment offered an exceptional incentive. Upon mustering into service the fourth company, or enlisting at least 292 men, the captain would take command of the independent battalion with the "rank, pay and emoluments of a lieutenant-colonel of infantry."[17]

The liberal terms offered to the Mormons were in keeping with Polk's desire to conciliate the followers of Brigham Young. Enlisted men were to choose their own officers, a captain and a first, second, and third lieutenant, for each company. Volunteers would be allowed to retain their guns and accoutrements "as their own property" at the end of their service. And each company would be permitted to enroll four women "with rations and other allowances" as laundresses.

At Council Bluffs, Henry W. Bigler on June 30 noted that a "Captain Allen and four others with a baggage wagon rolled into our camp, inquiring for Brigham Young."[18] The thirty-year-old Mormon emi-

---

[15] J. C. Edwards to W. L. Marcy, August 11, 1846, in Frank A. Golder, ed., *The March of the Mormon Battalion from Council Bluffs to California, Taken from the Journal of Henry Standage* (New York: The Century Co., 1928), 97.

[16] S. W. Kearny to J. Allen, June 19, 1846, in Golder, *Standage*, 101–2.

[17] Ibid.

[18] Erwin G. Gudde, *Bigler's Chronicle of the West, The Conquest of California, Discovery of Gold, and Mormon Settlement as Reflected in Henry William Bigler's Diaries* (Berkeley: University of California Press, 1962), 16–17.

grant was about to find out that inattentive staff work in the War Department could have drastic consequences for the average citizen who just wants to get along and mind his or her own business.

The next day, when he addressed the assembled camp, Allen had good reason to strike a positive note and make a good impression on his listeners. His offer was even better in the eyes of Mormon leaders who had given up, three weeks before, any hope of leading their people across the mountains that season. What they urgently needed was permission to settle for a time on Indian lands, which the captain took it upon himself to grant.

But a temporary resting place was only the most immediate of benefits the enlistment opportunity could provide. It also opened a way to move at least 500 followers to the West Coast at government expense. It would relieve the pressure from hundreds of wagons and thousands of emigrants crowding the camps and trails across Iowa. And this was still not all.

According to one emigrant, the Mormons before leaving Nauvoo had "entered into covenant to assist one anothe[r] till all the Saints got out of that place."[19] The pledge of mutual aid appeared to justify Brigham Young in the view that the pay and allowances of the soldiers could be collected and applied to the welfare of all.

So it was that Young followed Captain Allen to the wagon stand that day to propose that "five hundred volunteers be mustered," vowing to care for the families of the soldiers and "feed them when I had anything to eat myself."[20] Young then walked out himself "as recruiting sergeant" with his clerk and took some names. Later, he said, "we will call out the companies, and if there are not young men enough, we will take the old men, and if there are not enough, we will take the women."[21]

Not all were "healthy, able-bodied men of from eighteen to forty-five years of age,"[22] as specified on June 26 in his Circular to the Mormons, but the captain soon had more than enough soldiers to

---

[19] Journal of Albert Smith, 1804–1889 (typescript in possession of the editor prepared from photocopy of original journal located in the Historical Department, Church of Jesus Christ of Latter-day Saints, Salt Lake City).

[20] Journal History, in Golder, *Standage*, 109–10.

[21] Ibid., 121.

[22] Circular to the Mormons from J. Allen, Captain First Dragoons, June 26, 1846, in Golder, *Standage*, 102–3.

qualify him for the new rank of lieutenant colonel. The volunteers included a reluctant Virginian, Henry Bigler. Among others, Young's clerk had also taken down the names of a forty-one-year-old New Yorker, Albert Smith, and his son, Azariah, not quite eighteen.

Brigham Young later came to believe, or so he said, that the call for volunteers was part of a plot, hatched by Missouri Senator Thomas Hart Benton, to exterminate the members of the young faith as they headed into the wilderness. Under this design, Mormon leaders were expected to reject the "tyrannical requisition," at which President Polk was to call on the governors of Iowa, Missouri, and Illinois for troops to "march against us and massacre us all."[23] Fortunately for his followers, however, Young had seen through the devilish conspiracy and foiled it by a ringing demonstration of patriotism.

Battalion veteran Albert Smith would later echo this view in a statement, "Uncle Sam and the Mormon Battalion," apparently written at the time of the Civil War:

After "driving the Saints from Nauvoo, he demanded 500 men [to] serve in his army against New Mexico thinking that we [would] not go, and then calculating to cry treason Treason, and [se]nd his own men and kill us all off, en mass, but God through [His] Prophets, sent the Battallion according to his demand and saved [us] [fr]om his power."[24]

Out of this unlikely scenario came the historical tradition that the Mormon Battalion was a "ram in the thicket," like the animal Abraham discovered caught by the horns and sacrificed instead of his son, Isaac (Genesis 23:9–14). In much the same way, the legend goes, the volunteers had been offered as a sacrifice to save their people "from the evils designed by their enemies."[25]

The real story, that the soldiers were called because an enterprising coreligionist played on a president's fears that the British were coming and that an American commander misunderstood an ambig-

---

[23] Daniel Tyler, *A Concise History of the Mormon Battalion in the Mexican War, 1846-1847* (Salt Lake City, 1881), 351–55.

[24] Undated statement in possession of the editor, handwritten and signed by Albert Smith, which concludes: "And now Uncle you may fight one another [until] like the Killkeney cats you are all used up but the tail."

[25] Tyler, *Concise History*, 353.

uous order from the secretary of war,[26] takes nothing from the personal sacrifice of those who volunteered—their contribution to the Mormon emigration—and the historic march they made from Council Bluffs on the Missouri River to the Pacific shore to secure California for the United States.[27]

---

[26] First to point to the misunderstanding that led to the call of the Mormon Battalion was W. Ray Luce whose article, "The Mormon Battalion: A Historical Accident?" appeared in *Utah Historical Quarterly* 42 (Winter 1974).

[27] For the most complete work on the Mormon Battalion, see John F. Yurtinus, *A Ram in the Thicket: The Mormon Battalion in the Mexican War*, 2 vols. (Ph.D. thesis, Brigham Young University, 1975). Other studies include B. H. Roberts, *The Mormon Battalion, Its History and Achievements* (Salt Lake City: Deseret News, 1919); Bernard DeVoto, *The Year of Decision, 1846* (Boston: Little, Brown and Company, 1943); and Kate B. Carter, *The Mormon Battalion* (Salt Lake City: Daughters of Utah Pioneers, 1956).

1

BY THE CIMARRON TO
SANTA FE
August 1–October 16, 1846

Fort Leavenworth had already guarded the American frontier for
nearly twenty years when Azariah Smith marched in on August 1,
1846, his eighteenth birthday. But not in its long history would the
Missouri River post see another body of aspiring soldiers like the
volunteers who reported for duty that day.

Ranging in age from youths in their teens to white-bearded grand-
fathers, the arrivals represented a cross section of the refugees who
filled Mormon emigration camps in Iowa. Many, like young Smith's
father, were married men with dependent children. Some rode in
wagons, too sick to walk. And one had already died on the short march
from Council Bluffs.

At least thirty-six of the recruits, unwilling to leave their families
on the plains, had brought their wives with them; at least twenty of
the women enrolled by special permission of the army as laundresses.
The cavalcade also included as many as fifty children and an unspeci-
fied number of other family members and camp followers of all ages.
All told, it added up to more than 600 individuals.

Only five weeks before, the proud First Missouri Mounted Volunteers under the regiment's new colonel, Alexander W. Doniphan, an
old friend of the Mormons, had marched from Fort Leavenworth with
the advance of the Army of the West to conquer New Mexico. Like
the thousands who flocked to the colors that summer at President Polk's
call, the Missourians were young, eager for adventure, and bursting

11

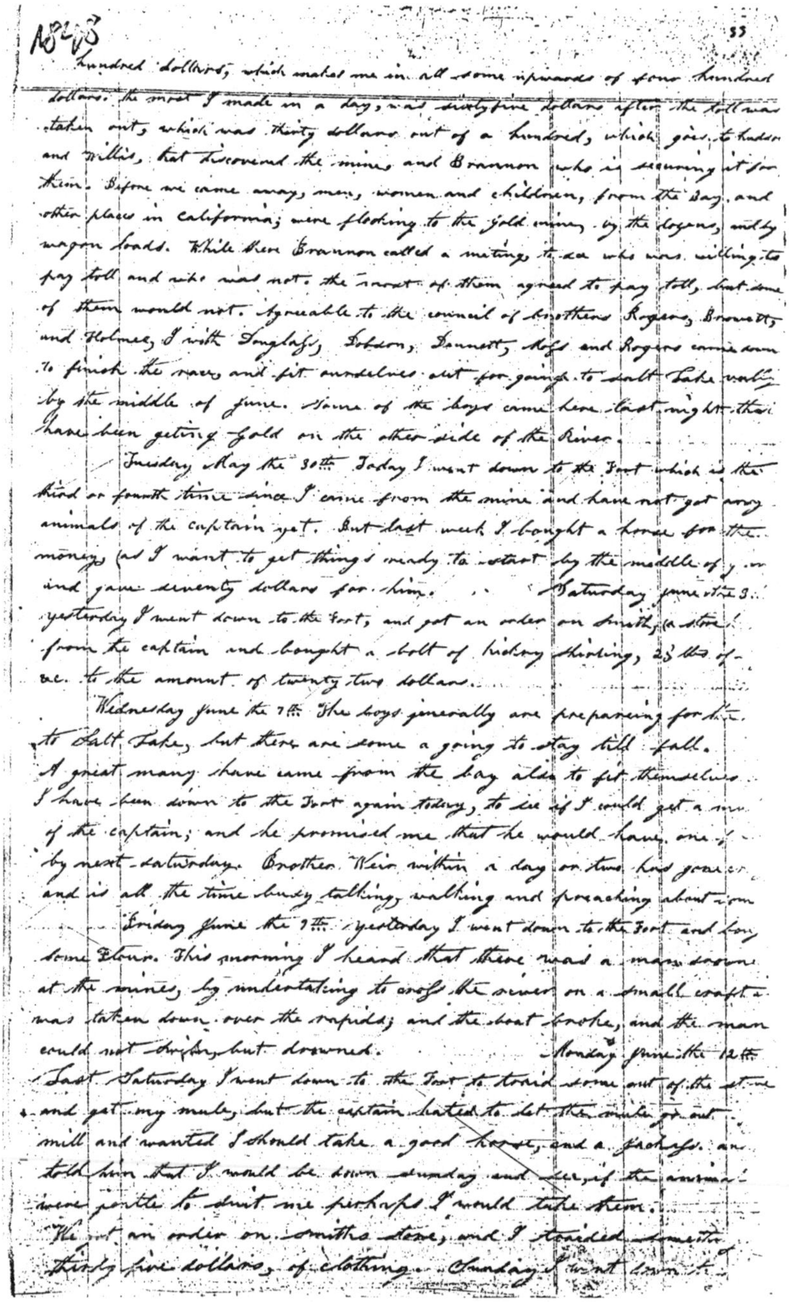
1848 33

hundred dollars, which makes me in all some upwards of four hundred dollars. the most I made in a day, was sixty five dollars after the toll was taken out, which was thirty dollars out of a hundred, which goes to Hudson and Willis, hat discovered the mine and Brannon who is securing it for them. Before we came away, men, women and children, from the Bay and other places in california; were flocking to the gold mines by the dozens, and by wagon loads. While there Brannon called a meting to see who was willing to pay toll and who was not. the most of them agreed to pay toll, but some of them would not. Agreeable to the council of brothers Rogers, Brownett, and Holmes, I with Douglass, Dobson, Dennett, Moss and Rogers came down to finish the race and fit ourselves out for going to Salt Lake valley by the middle of June. Some of the boys came here last night that have been geting gold on the other side of the River.

Tuesday May the 30th Today I went down to the Fort which is the third or fourth time since I came from the mine and have not got any animals of the captain yet. But last week I bought a horse for the money (as I want to get things ready to start by the middle of J[illegible] and gave seventy dollars for him. Saturday June the 3 yesterday I went down to the Fort, and got an order on Smith (a store) from the captain and bought a bolt of hickory shirting, 23 lbs of [illegible] &c. to the amount of twenty two dollars.

Wednesday June the 7th The boys generally are preparing for the [illegible] to Salt Lake, but there are some a going to stay till fall. A great many have came from the bay also to fit themselves. I have been down to the Fort again today, to see if I could get a m[illegible] of the captain; and he promised me that he would have one [illegible] by next saturday. Brother Weir within a day or two has gone [illegible] and is all the time busy talking, walking and preaching about [illegible]

Friday June the 9th yesterday I went down to the Fort and [illegible] some flour. This morning I heard that there was a man drown[illegible] at the mines, by undertaking to cross the river on a small craft [illegible] was taken down over the rapids; and the boat broke, and the man could not swim, but drowned. Monday June the 12th Last Saturday I went down to the Fort to trade some out of the store and get my mule, but the captain hated to let the mule go out [illegible] mill and wanted I should take a good horse, and a jackass. [illegible] told him that I would be down sunday and see if the animals were gentle to suit me perhaps I would take them. [illegible] got an order on Smiths store, and I traded something [illegible] thirty five dollars, of clothing. Sunday I went down to [illegible]

Handwritten page from the 1848 journal of Azariah Smith.

with patriotism. Wrote one ardent Clay County volunteer: "we are for our country right or wrong."[1]

But the volunteering spirit that swept most parts of the country at the start of the War with Mexico hardly reflected the mood of the nearly 500 Mormon recruits, already formed into a battalion of five companies, A through E, who drew their muskets on August 3. Most had already seen conflict enough during earlier religious wars in Missouri and Illinois. All they wanted now was to find a place to live in peace and put their unique beliefs into practice without outside interference.

Many were also deeply bitter at the failure of the American republic to protect their religious rights and resentful at being called to serve such a government. Not uncommon were the feelings of the elder Smith who wrote: "For government to mak[e] Such a demand when we ware driven from our homes & Possesions & were scattred upon the plains from Nauvoo to the Mosurie river was more Cruel than the Grave."[2]

Given their turbulent history and impoverished condition, few of the Mormons would have volunteered that year for any reason other than to obey the "counsel" laid down by their leaders.

Twelve months later, it would be ironic that a quarter of the battalion members who made it to California ignored such direction and reenlisted for six months, while the Missourians of the First Mounted Regiment in the very face of the enemy, deep in Mexico, refused to a man to extend their service by even a day.

At Fort Leavenworth, each new arrival received a heavy flintlock musket and enough equipment on belts and straps to cover him up "from neck to waist," according to Company E recruit Zodak Judd. It included a cartridge box "with heavy leather belt two and one fourth inches wide to carry over the left shoulder," another big belt with "bayonet and scabbard attached" to carry over the right shoulder, and a belt "correspondingly wide and heavy all white leather" to wear around his waist. In addition, he was given a knap-

---

[1] John Edward Weems, *To Conquer a Peace, The War between the United States and Mexico* (Garden City, N.Y.: Doubleday & Company, 1974), which includes quotes from the diary of John T. Hughes.

[2] Journal of Albert Smith, 1804–1889, July 2, 1846 (referred to hereafter as Albert Smith Journal).

sack to carry his clothing, "so arranged that a strap came in from each shoulder and under the arm with a long strap to reach around our bedding," a half-gallon canteen, pint cup, clothing, blankets, twenty-four rounds of ammunition, and a haversack, or dinner bag, "made to swing over our shoulders also."[3] All told, it amounted to "A hevy load for a Mule," complained Albert Smith.[4]

And they prepared to carry out their assigned mission to support Stephen W. Kearny in the conquest of New Mexico and California without benefit of any drill or military instruction important enough for anyone to take note of.[5] For Azariah Smith, "the first time that I ever was taught how to turn around" would not come until he was on occupation duty in California, six months later.

Meanwhile, harmful to morale in the beginning was the unexpected death on August 23 of the battalion's respected first commander, Lieutenant Colonel James Allen, who took to the grave whatever promises he had made to Brigham Young as to the leadership succession and the handling of the Mormon troops and civilian camp followers.

Allen's temporary successor, First Lieutenant Andrew Jackson Smith of the First Dragoons, was to demonstrate at this stage of his long and distinguished military career that he had much to learn about citizen soldiers and how to lead them. By the time he took command, the most remarkable body of infantry ever to march from Fort Leavenworth was already well along on the first leg of its journey—the 820-mile road to Santa Fe.

Over the next two years, Azariah Smith would travel more than 3,000 miles and take part in some of the most decisive events in American history. He begins his story of these adventures, as they happened,

---

[3] Autobiography of Zodak Knapp Judd, typewritten copy at Utah State Historical Society, 19.

[4] Albert Smith Journal, August 5, 1846.

[5] For more on Stephen W. Kearny's Army of the West, see Ralph P. Bieber, ed., *Journal of a Soldier under Kearny and Doniphan, 1846–1847* (Glendale, Calif.: Arthur H. Clark Co., 1935); Ralph P. Bieber, ed., *Marching with the Army of the West, 1846–1848* (Glendale, Calif.: Arthur H. Clark Co., 1936); and Robert Selph Henry, *The Story of the Mexican War* (Indianapolis: Bobbs-Merrill Company, 1950).

with a brief account of his life before entering the U.S. Army as a private in Company B of the Mormon Battalion.[6]

[The Journal]

I was born, New York State, Oswego County, Town of Boilston, August, 1st. 1828, of Albert, and Esther Dutcher.[7] When I was seven years old, we moved to the State of Ohio. In the year, 1839, Father and Mother embraced the Church of Latter day Saints. And then it being Council from God, we started for the State of Missouria, But when we got to Sangamon County, Illinois, on account of the Saints being driven out of the State of Missouria at the point of the bayonet, a great many men, women and children being killed by the Mob, we therefore, stoped in Sangamon County, Illinois, and lived there with a small Branch [until] the year 1840. When the Saints, were again gathering, at a place called Commerce, on the banks of the Mississippi River, Hancock County, Illinois. We then moved to that place, but moved on the other Side of the Mississippi River, in the Iowa Territory, and, lived there about one year.[8]

And while we lived there, in the year 1841, I was Baptised into the Church. During the year, 1841, after building a house we moved back to Commerce, (afterwards the city of Nauvoo, And was afterwards again changed [to] the City of Joseph.) We then lived there assisting in building up the place, the Temple being a Splendid Build-

---

[6] For the best source on the makeup of the battalion, see Carl V. Larson, *A Data Base of the Mormon Battalion, An Identification of the Original Members of the Mormon Battalion* (Providence, Utah: Keith W. Watkins and Sons Printing, 1987). Also see Elmer J. Carr, ed., *Honorable Remembrance, The San Diego Master List of the Mormon Battalion* (San Diego: Mormon Battalion Visitors Center, 1972–78).

[7] Like many Mormons of that period, Azariah's parents came from the Lake Ontario region of New York where the new American faith had its beginnings. They were later among the first settlers of Manti, Utah.

[8] The Smiths apparently located on land acquired by Mormon prophet Joseph Smith from one Isaac Galland, a promoter and swindler, who forged deeds to the Iowa property, known as the Half-Breed Tract, which he did not own. As a result, many families in 1841 lost their farms and moved across the river to Nauvoo, the Mormon metropolis on the eastern shore in Hancock County, Illinois.

ing, built by the Saints, of Lime Stone, according to a pattern given by Revelation from God, to Joseph Smith as also other Buildings, to build up the place.

We also had me[e]tings, where we received teachings, pertaining [to] eternal life; from the Prophets, Apostles, and others in authority, also recieving revelations through the men apointed, from time to time, which often gladened the heart.

Joseph Smith, and Hyrum his Brother, the former the Prophet, and the latter Patriarch, of the Church of, Jesus Christ, of latter day Saints, were shot in Carthage Jail on the 27th. of June, 1844, about five 0 clock P.M., by an armed mob, painted black of 150 to 200 persons. Hyrum was Shot first calmly exclaiming "I am a dead man!" Joseph [leaped] from the window, and was Shot dead in the act exclaiming "O Lord my God!" They were [also shot] after they were dead in brutal manner, and each recieved four balls. John Taylor[9] and Willard Richards,[10] two of the Twelve, were the only persons in the room at the time. The former was wounded in savage manner with four balls, but has since recovered, the latter, through the promises of God escaped "without even a hole in his robe."

I am sure that I never felt worse, than at that time. Brigham Young, who was then president of the Quorum of the Twelve, took the place of presiding over the Church, with the unction of the church. The Temple was then finished sufficient for giveing endowments, which Father and Mother recieved a portion, in due Season.

As the people of the State, and of the United, (or divided,) States, were not willing, for us to remain in peace, continally trying their dexterity, at mobbing, and trying to destroy the Saints from the face of the earth. In the year 1846, according to the command of the Lord, the Church removed into the Wilderness. Father went with

---

[9] Apostle Taylor, then thirty-five, survived the slaughter at Carthage Jail and went on to become the third president of the Mormon faith after the death of Brigham Young in 1877. He died at Kaysville, Utah, ten years later.

[10] Forty-year-old Richards fought off the muskets of attackers with his walking stick to escape unhurt from the murderous assault. Before his death in 1854, the New Englander served as counselor to Brigham Young, postmaster of Salt Lake City, and editor of the church-owned *Deseret News*.

the Pioneers, but I stayed at home, with the rest of the family, till we finally started with Brother Dame,[11] not haveing any team, of our own, I driving team.

While on the ways we met Father, comeing back after us. After geting to Pisgah,[12] we stoped and built us a house, got in some garden sauce, corn, &c, but haveing an opportunity we left it, and again, with elder Woodruff,[13] started on, and upon ariving at Council Bluffs,[14] Missouria River, there were United States officers there, after Mormon volunteers, for a Battalion. The council of the heads of the Church was to the Saints, to volunteer, upon which, the Battalion was made up. I and Father[15] and Thomas P Dutcher, (Mothers brother,) were three of the number that enlisted.[16]

---

[11] This was either Janvrin H. Dame, then thirty-six, a native of Farmington, New Hampshire, or his twenty-five-year-old nephew, William H. Dame, who later settled in southern Utah where he commanded the military district when Mormons and Indians in 1857 massacred some 120 Arkansas emigrants at a place on the southern trail to California known as Mountain Meadows. Janvrin Dame in 1852 was among the earliest settlers of Fillmore, Utah.

[12] Mount Pisgah, a major staging area in the Mormon movement across Iowa, was located near present Talmage, about nineteen miles west of Osceola.

[13] Wilford Woodruff, then thirty-nine, born near Hartford, Conn., and ordained an apostle at age thirty-two, became fourth president of the Mormon Church in 1889. A year later he issued the historic manifesto that abolished the practice of polygamy and cleared the way for Utah statehood. He died in 1898 at age ninety-one.

[14] Council Bluffs, located on the left bank of the Missouri River, opposite present Omaha, Nebr., was the temporary terminus of the Mormon emigration in 1846.

[15] When Albert Smith enlisted, he and his wife, Esther, thirty-five, were the parents of four children with seventeen-year-old Azariah the oldest and the youngest less than two years of age. He was named third sergeant of Company B in which Azariah served as a private.

[16] Born in Cherry Valley, N.Y., Thomas P. Dutcher reenlisted for six months in 1847 and later moved to Portland, Mich., where he was a member of the Reorganized L.D.S. Church which followed Joseph Smith, III, the first prophet's oldest son.

[July 22-August 8, 1846]

We arived at Fort Levenworth,[17] after a spe[e]dy travail from the bluffs. We had a very good time excepting its being very warm. There was one man died on the road.[18] On the 22nd. Brother Little[19] [bl]essed us. Thomas was also taken Sick on the way. July the 30th. We had a heavy wind storm which blew the trees down in every direction. On the 31st. We marched through WeStun[20] with music at the head; we travailed four miles & washed in the afternoon. August 1st. My birth day we marched into Fort Levenworth. August 3rd. We drawed our Muskets. August 5th. We receaved 42. Dollars each for our years clothing. August 6th. I sent 20 Dollars to Mother, and one to the Twelve, bought some Clothing and a canteen.[21] August 7th. The weather is warm and Thomas is very Sick. August 8th. Yesterday we drawed our Napsacks and dinner Bags, which I think just makes out a good harness for a mule. Today we recieved a days rations.

---

[17] Fort Leavenworth, near present Kansas City, is the oldest U.S. Army post west of the Mississippi River still in existence and the most famous in the history of the West with the possible exception of Fort Laramie. It was founded on the right bank of the Missouri River in 1827 by Colonel Henry Leavenworth, Third U.S. Infantry, to protect the Santa Fe Trail.

[18] Private Samuel Boley, Company B, praised the day before for his "energy and integrity," died of an unnamed illness early on the third day of the march from Council Bluffs. He was the first of twenty battalion members or teamsters to die in service. See Tyler, *Concise History*, 131.

[19] Jesse C. Little, whose letter to President Polk won approval for the enlistment of Mormon volunteers to serve in California, has never received the credit he deserves for his role in preserving the Mormon movement in 1846. After serving as adjutant of the pioneer company to Utah in 1847, the New Englander moved west permanently in 1852 and died at Salt Lake City at the age of seventy-eight.

[20] At Weston, the command came within a few miles of Jackson County, designated by the Mormon prophet as the location of Zion, scene of a confrontation in 1833 between members of the faith and old settlers that later spread to other western Missouri counties. The conflict culminated in the so-called Mormon War of 1838 and the expulsion of Joseph Smith's followers from the state in 1839.

[21] Much of the money soldiers sent to families was delivered to Brigham Young who considered it a "manifestation of the kind providence of our Heavenly Father . . . just in time for the purchase of provisions and goods for the winter supply of the camp." See B. Young to Mormon Battalion, August 20, 1846, Journal History; Golder, *Standage*, 143–45.

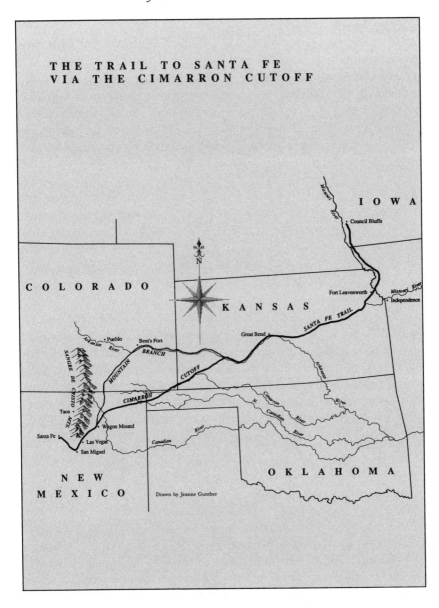

THE TRAIL TO SANTA FE
VIA THE CIMARRON CUTOFF

Sunday the 9th. Warm and pleasant Thomas is geting better.

Monday the 10th. Father went to Western [Weston] and I stayed with Thomas; it was hot enough to melt Cheese. We have now two span of mules, instead of cattle to draw our Napsacks.

[August 11–14, 1846]

Tuesday the 11th. We lay in camp. Wednesday the 12th. We packed up ready to start the next morning. Thursday Aug 13th. We started at one oclock, with our muskets and equipments, and music at the head. We marched 5 miles and encamped. Our Provision wagon broke and we had to go with out our Supper. Friday Aug the 14th. Colonel Allen, Sent us another wagon and this morning it arived at camp. We stayed there till one oclock, and then struck our tents and travailed 4 miles and then encamped for night.

[August 15–17, 1846]

Saturday Aug 15th. Last night I stood guard and travailed twelve, or thirteen miles. Sunday Aug 16th. We crossed the Canzah it being 40, miles from the fort.[22] Monday the 17th. The company [searched for] Cattle there being 35 head lost. We also had washing done.

[August 19–21, 1846]

Wednesday Aug 19th. Yesterday we had a fine Shower for our [relief]. Today it was wet & rainy, but at noon we started and travailed [four] miles, and just as we got our tents pitched there came a [sudden storm] of wind and rain; it blew our tents over, and us in a pile; it hailed also considerable. Thursday Aug the 20th. We hung out our N[apsacks] and cloths, to dry, and cleaned our guns. In the afternoon we h[eld] me[e]ting. Friday the 21st. Was spent in pitching dollars, and [other kinds] of amusement. Ajitant Dikes[23] arived today at camp.

----

[22] The Kansas River crossing was near Fish's Ferry, a few miles east of present Lawrence, Kans.

[23] Lieutenant George P. Dykes, thirty-one, the most disliked of the Mormon officers, was named on Brigham Young's recommendation the battalion's first adjutant. He later resigned under fire from fellow religionists who resented his enforcing the orders of non-Mormon officers, especially those of U.S. Army Surgeon George B. Sanderson that required soldiers to take accepted medicines of the day rather than rely on herbs or the laying on of hands to cure their ailments. Called "Dr. Death" by religious zealots in the command, an insult unfairly repeated by historians ever since, Sanderson was trusted by regular army officers and was probably as capable as most physicians of that period. That he was not hated or resented by either young Smith or his father does credit to their good sense.

[August 22-25, 1846]

Saturday Aug 22nd. Last night I stood guard, and travailed 15 miles, and pitched our tents at Elm Grove.[24] Sunday the 23rd. Trav[ailed] 24 miles. Monday Aug 24th. Travailed 14 miles. Tuesday the [25th.] This morning Brother [Mc]Kenzy met us going to the Bluffs.[25]

Wednesday Aug 26th. We travailed till noon then stoped to [recover], when a wagon loaded with flour, women and Sick [turned] over into a creek. We travailed till night and encamped.

Thursday the 27th. We recieved news from the fort that Colonel James Allen had died.[26] We travailed till 1 oclock.

Friday Aug the 28th. Last night Sister Bosco[27] died. This [day I] bought a shirt, and—some socks.

---

[24] At Elm Grove, near present Baldwin City, Kans., the command took up its line of march on the Santa Fe Trail, an established artery of commerce for a quarter century. The route and its Cimarron Cutoff, followed by the battalion, are paralleled today, but seldom traced exactly, by U.S. Highway 56 across Kansas, the Oklahoma Panhandle, and eastern New Mexico.

[25] McKenzie, identified as a Mormon, was returning from a trading mission to Santa Fe. He was on his way from Bent's Fort to the Mormon emigration camp at Council Bluffs.

[26] Beyond his Ohio birth and military record, little is known about Lieutenant Colonel James Allen, about forty, the battalion's first commander. Also obscure is the cause of his sudden death on August 23 from an illness identified only as "congestive fever." Henry Bigler, Company B, darkly suggested the possibility that Allen had been poisoned by someone who feared he was too friendly to the Mormons. One hundred thirty-one years after his death, Allen finally won the recognition he deserved when the Veterans Administration in special services at Fort Leavenworth National Cemetery in 1977 replaced his gravestone, which had listed him as captain, with a new stone reporting his true and official rank of lieutenant colonel. See Gudde, *Bigler's Chronicle*, 23. Also see Harold Schindler, "Rites Honor LDS Friend," *Salt Lake Tribune*, September 16, 1977.

[27] Jane Bosco became reunited in death with her husband, John, not a member of the command, who had died only two days before. Seldom separated, the couple were members of Jefferson Hunt's family who had followed the battalion in the hope of reaching California under its protection.

[August, 29-30, 1846]

Saturday Aug the 29th. This morning the Sun shines most bieutifull and glorius, I bought a pair of pantaloons. Evenings we meet at the Captains tent and have prairs. At one oclock the Drum beat and we all marched down in a Grove, by Council Grove Creek,[28] and heard a funeral sermon preached by Ajitant Dikes, upon the death of Colonel James Allen, and the reserection, followed by Captain Hunt,[29] and me[e]ting closed by father Pedigrew.[30] This evening Mr. Pomroy, (the Colonel's waiter) and also Mr. Smith[31] arived at Camp. Some recieved letters from the Bluffs. Sunday August 30th. I have been a bakeing up bread expecting to start at 9 or 10 oclock. P.M.

---

[28] Council Grove takes its name from treaty negotiations with the Osage tribe in 1824 to ensure safe passage of the Neosho River for caravans on the trail to Santa Fe. Later, freighters stopped here to cut wood for spare axles and form trains for defense against Indians. It is today a scenic location on U.S. Highway 56 in Morris County, Kans.

[29] Senior Mormon officer, Captain Jefferson Hunt of Company A, then forty-three, had been a leader of Zionist forces in Missouri and Illinois. When he volunteered, the lean Kentuckian took his whole family with him, including his first wife, Celia, a second wife, Matilda, two sons, Gilbert and Marshall, who also enlisted in Company A, four other sons, and three daughters.

[30] David Pettegrew, oldest at fifty-five to complete the march to California, was a leader of an extremist faction that often disputed the secular authority of more moderate Mormon officers and made the battalion's history a chronicle of backbiting and dissent. Only a private, he had been told by Brigham Young himself to enlist, "it being a particular request," and called on by the officers "to take charge of the spiritual affairs of the camp," a broad mandate in those days. The zealous Vermont native died at Salt Lake City in 1863. See Autobiography and Journal of David Pettegrew, 1840–1860, typed copy prepared by the editor in 1964 from the original handwritten manuscript, then owned by Mrs. Virginia Kelson of Salt Lake City, and donated to the Utah State Historical Society (referred to hereafter as Pettegrew Journal, 69–70).

[31] First Lieutenant Andrew Jackson Smith came from Fort Leavenworth to offer his services as commander of the battalion until a successor to Lieutenant Colonel Allen could be named. The young Pennsylvanian later became a major general during the Civil War and in 1866 was named first colonel of the new Seventh Cavalry which found fame on the Little Big Horn River in 1876 under its second in command, Lieutenant Colonel George A. Custer.

The orders of the morning have been ratified, and we are to start tomorrow morning at 9 oclock. There have been, and is still a great many sick, but we pray to the Lord to raise them up. As for me I am well for which I feel gratefull to him who grants me this blessing. It is a beautifull evening and I with some of the rest of the Company went up on a mountain and got stones and caried them to the graves of Bosco and his wife, and built a wall around the graves 10 feet by 7 Square and filled it up level inside.

Monday Aug the 31st. This morning after haveing called the roll, and a rear guard, we marched till about 2 oclock and camped for night by Diamond Spring.[32] We are now under command of Colonel Smith.[33] This evening we had a muster of the whole Battalion.

[September 1–4, 1846]

Tuesday Sept 1st. 1846. Last night and this morning we baked bread to last us two days, there being no wood for thirty miles. I and Thomas went ahead this morning as my eyes were so sore that I could not travail in the dust of the Battalion. We travailed 15. miles and camped by a Spring on the prairy called the Lost Spring.[34] We arived at the Spring about 2 oclock, dry and dusty; there is no wood here. A horse Co. travailed just before us today.[35] Wednesday the 2nd. It

---

[32] Diamond Springs, located in the southwestern corner of present Morris County, Kans., was named for the sparkling quality of its water.

[33] Lacking credentials and experience, the Mormon officers reluctantly approved Smith to command the force as far as Santa Fe. Like many regular army officers of that day, he proved to be a hard disciplinarian whose accession to command stirred widespread resentment among the volunteers. It also proved contrary to the will of Brigham Young who wanted a Mormon officer, Jefferson Hunt, to take over as commander of the battalion.

[34] Lost Springs, located near the present town of the same name in Marion County, was difficult to find because there were no trees to mark its location.

[35] The Mormon infantry shared the trail with the Second Regiment of Missouri Mounted Volunteers under Colonel Sterling Price who would later command at Santa Fe and in 1848 mount an expedition into northern Mexico during the closing days of the war. The Missourians and their commander were roundly hated by the Mormons for the role they played as state militia in driving the religionists from Missouri in 1838–39. Price later became a major general in the Confederate Army.

rained a little this morning to lay the dust and made fine travailing. At two or three oclock we camped and I baked bread till 10 oclock at night.[36] Thursday Sept. 3d. This morning I baked some more bread and to day we travailed about 25 miles. I got prety tired. Friday Sept. 4th. Last night we had considerable rain. It sprinkled through the tents and made our blankets quite wet. We packed up early and I went ahead and got to the little Canzas[37] an hour or two first. After I started, it was cloudy and sprinkled some, but after a little, it cleared and the Sun came out and shone bright and made fine travailing. We camped at the Canzas and had some fried cakes for sup[p]er.

Sunday Sept. the 6th. Yesterday I went ahead and stood it first rate, and when I got to a creek, I picked Some grapes, and this morning I made some wine. This morning, I was deta[i]lled for guard, we stayed till the Battalion had all left, and then we started in the rear. After we had travailed 2 or 3 miles, we saw a man comeing off from the prairy. We waited till he came, and he had a piece of a buffalo. He said he saw three, he had loaded his rifle when horsemen came over the hills. They killed one of them, and he got a piece.

We marched till 6 or 7, oclock, and had some Buffalo meat and fried cakes for supper. Monday the 7th. I stood guard last night, and again this morning; stayed till the Battalion had all left. We got very cold but after we started we got warm. We started without our breakfast there being no wood or water. Being the rear guard we did not get to camp till 2. or 3, oclock. We were then dismissed and had a first rate supper consisting of Buffalo pot pie. Some of the men wounded a Buffalo, five or six, miles from camp and then drove him in, and killed him.

---

[36] While Azariah baked bread, Albert Smith noted on this date: "There is in our company too Cannons drawn by 6 horses each one black-smith shop drown by 6 horses (40) forty provision wagons & wagons with twelve familyes & 12 wagons belonging to the Sutters or traders besides the bagage wagons [which] belong to us." See Albert Smith Journal, September 2, 1846.

[37] This river was the Little Arkansas, crossed at a point about twenty miles north of present Hutchinson, Kans.

Tuesday Sept the 8th. I took Sergeant Corays[38] team to drive; after breakfast we started. I liked my harbour first rate for it rained all day. Today we Saw Thousands of Buffalo, and there were [a] few killed. Wednesday Sept. the 9th. Last night we arrived at a creek that was so high, that we did not cross. We went up the creek a [mile] and camped. I staked out the mules, and pitched the tent in the [rain]. I am now in Sergeant Corays mess. This evening I harnessed up. We crossed the creek, (which is called Pawne[e] Fork,)[39] and went about 5 miles and camped on Pawne[e] Fork. It is the most beautifull prairy I ever Saw. I have been helping Sister Coray wash, and it looks like rain.

Thursday the 10th. Last night we had a heavy gale of wind which blew down the tents. Today we travailed on a beautifull Prairy, and saw plenty of Buffalo.[40]

---

[38] William Coray was the twenty-three-year-old first sergeant of Company B. His wife, Melissa, eighteen, was one of only four women who made the entire march from Council Bluffs to California. The others were Susan Davis, wife of Captain Daniel C. Davis; Phoebe Brown, wife of Sergeant Ebenezer Brown; and Lydia Hunter, who died at San Diego, wife of Captain Jesse D. Hunter. Melissa Burton Coray, then surnamed Kimball, said in 1901 that the wife of Private Eleaser Davis, no first name given, also completed the journey, but there is no confirmation of this other than Cooke's admission that he had "reluctantly consented" to take five women along "at their own expense." See "Utah Woman's 2,000-mile March Fifty-five Years Ago," *Salt Lake Herald*, May 26, 1901, 2. Also see *Official Journal of Lieutenant Colonel Philip St. George Cooke, From Santa Fe to San Diego, Etc.*, October 13, 1846, Sen. Doc. 2, 30th Cong., spec. sess., 1849 (referred to hereafter as Cooke's Journal).

[39] The battalion struck the Pawnee River near its junction with the Arkansas River, not far from present Larned, Kans., and moved a short distance up the swollen stream to find a crossing.

[40] Smith fails to note that orders arrived on this day for the battalion to take the more direct route to New Mexico, known as the Cimarron Cut-off, rather than go to Santa Fe on the Mountain Branch of the trail, followed earlier by General Kearny and his command. The latter route continued up the Arkansas River along the present line of U.S. Highway 50 to Bent's Fort, near present LaJunta, Colo., then turned south through Raton Pass to meet the Cimarron road near present Watrous, N.M., about eighty miles from Santa Fe.

Friday Sept. the 11th. Last night we had to use Buffalo chips for fuel, haveing no wood. We had a beautifull day and travailed to the Arcanzas River[41] where [we] encamped. We crossed the river on foot and got wood, there being [wood] only in places. Plenty to eat at present.

Saturday the [12th.] After the revellee this morning we started, and travailed 20 miles up the river and camped on its banks. It [was a] level plain of sand entirely across and we had to [dig] in the Sand to get water.

Sunday Sept the 13th. This morning as usial we travailed up the river and encamped on the banks of the same, haveing to dig holes in the Sand for water as before.

Monday Sept 14th. We had a fine road today, and travailed about 18 miles & encamped on the banks of the river. The road in some places was white as chawk, some call it lime; other plaster paris. The prairy is all over like a pasture, with bones and Buffalo sculls all over. The times go very well with me except my eyes being very Sore. This morning I went over on the Island after wood, where there was logs built up, where Indians had lived some time.

Tuesday the 15th. We travailed today 15 miles, and crossed the river and camped by it on the other side, haveing to go a mile and a half after wood, I got on a mule and went after some. I got a stick on my shoulder, and got on the mule, but the mule threw me off and went to camp; it hurt me some, but not Seriously. Comeing back I saw a rattlesnake, which is the first one I have saw on the road.[42]

---

[41] Although the command for several days had marched within a dozen miles of the Arkansas River, it first camped on that waterway near present Kinsley, Kans., on U.S. Highway 56.

[42] Rattlesnakes were the least of the nuisances found at this camp, near present Ingalls, Kans., where the Cimarron Cutoff left the Arkansas River to begin a fifty-mile *jornada* across the treeless prairie to the headwaters of the Cimarron River. The Mormons were forced to bivouac near five companies of Missourians whom they regarded as a "profane, wicked and vulgar set of men."

Wednesday Sept. the 16th. This morning I was detailed for guard expecting to start forthwith and travail 25 miles today, (there being no water for fifty miles) but my back being sore I was released. I harnessed up all ready to start when orders came that we would not start till tomorrow morning. Today the families that have came with us so far have started for Bents Fort, where they calculate to winter. Some men went with them for guard.[43]

Friday the 18th. Yesterday we travailed 25 miles on a beautifull Prairy, and camped, without wood or water.[44] This morning we started early and travailed late Seeing plenty of Buffalo. We camped by a pond, where we watered ourselves and mules; a good many mules and oxen gave out to day, and some of the men had to go without their supper.

Saturday Sept. 19th. Today we travailed 8 miles to Diamond Spring.[45] The wind blew tremendiously and almost put out my eyes. I had to go about a half a mile after Buffalo chips to make a fire.

---

[43] Preparing to march into a hostile region, Lieutenant Smith ordered a number of family members, mainly wives and children, to go with an escort of ten enlisted men under forty-year-old Captain Nelson Higgins, via Bent's Fort, to the little settlement of Fort Pueblo, founded by trappers a few years before on the upper Arkansas River. There the battalion families joined at least sixty other members of the faith from Mississippi and southern Illinois who had chosen the place to winter after failing to meet the main Mormon emigration on the Platte River. Added to by later battalion detachments, the Pueblo colonists entered Great Salt Lake Valley five days after the arrival of Brigham Young's pioneer company in July 1847.

[44] Before moving out on the Cimarron Cutoff, Company E buried on the right bank of the Arkansas River Alva Phelps who died on September 16 after Battalion Surgeon Sanderson "with some horrid oaths" forced some "strong medicine" down his throat "with the old rusty spoon," according to Sergeant Tyler. Many in the company felt "the Doctor had killed him" and "that it was a case of premeditated murder." Phelps left a wife and two children at the Mormon camp in Iowa. See Tyler, *Concise History*, 158.

[45] At this place, properly named Wagon Bed Springs, or Lower Springs, the most renowned trapper and explorer in western history, Jedediah S. Smith, was killed in 1831 at the age of thirty-two by Comanche Indians. It is located near the confluence of the Cimarron River forks, normally dry during summer, near present Ulysses, Kans. Some think Smith was killed

Sunday Sept the 20th. This morning I did not start till all of the Battalion had left, Staying for Sergeant Coray to fix his wagon. We travailed ten or more miles and dug holes in the ground for water, and used Buffalo chips as before.

Monday Sept the 21st. Last night I was detaled for guard and marched with the guard all day, but my eyes being so sore, there was another man detaled to stand guard tonight in my place.

Wednesday the 23rd. Yesterday I drove Corays team. Last night an ox fell in a hole that was dug for water, and broke his neck. This morning I felt first rate; we had a sandy road all day and so[me] of the teams gave out on the way.[46]

Friday Sept the 25th. Yesterday we had a hard days travail, through the sand. On the prairy there was ninety mules heads all strung in a row which had froze to death, with travailers heretofore.[47] Today we had a first rate road, and passed through beautifull mountains, which looked as if volcanoes had been tearing there some time.

Saturday the 26th. 46 Today I have seen as much as 50 Antilope travailing on a beautifull prairy by myself. We camped by a creek

---

at an early waterhole, since washed out, known in its day as Wagon Body Springs, or Fargo Springs, some twenty-five miles downstream. For more on this, see Harry E. Chrisman, "Here They Killed Jed Smith," *1962 Brand Book of the Denver Posse of the Westerners*, 273–90.

[46] References to sandy conditions indicate that the battalion, for whatever reason, marched on the dry bed of the Cimarron River rather than follow a firmer road for wagons in the hills north of the waterway.

[47] This entry placed the command at Willow Bar, also known as Hundred Mule Heads, where Santa Fe trader Albert Speyer two years before had lost a hundred or more mules in an unseasonable snowstorm. For years after, a favorite prank of travelers on the Cimarron Cutoff was to arrange the bones of Speyer's mules in outlandish designs created to astonish, mystify, or amuse those who followed on the trail. The spot is now located on the Cimarron in the Oklahoma Panhandle, some ten miles north of Keyes, Okla., and two miles south of the Colorado line. See James Josiah Webb, *Adventures in the Santa Fe Trade, 1844–1847*, Ralph P. Bieber, ed. (Glendale, Calif.: Arthur H. Clark Company, 1931), 107.

Wagon Mound, New Mexico, last great landmark on the westward journey over the Cimarron Cutoff, where Mormon infantrymen camped before marching on to Santa Fe.

where there was no water;[48] and had to go about a half a mile after wood and water.

Sunday Sept. the 27th. Today I travailed on the prairy in order to shoot some Antilope with not much success. There is no wood or water here of any acount but the Battalion are all in good health, and spirits. This evening an express has been Sent to General Carna.[49]

Tuesday Sept. the 29th. Yesterday I shot 3 times at Antilope, [but] did not hit. Last night I came back into fathers mess again and today I shot an antilope, about 3 miles from camp, [and] I with two others packed it to camp.

October the 3d. For two or three days back we have travailed very fast. The [last] day of Sept. we travailed till 10. oclock and yesterday we travailed 23. miles. Today I went across and got ahead about 6 miles, [but] had to go back. When I got back they had volunteers to go to Santafee in Seven days, of which I and Father were two [of] that number.[50]

---

[48] They camped at or near McNee's Crossing of Corrumpa Creek, a headwater of the North Canadian River, named after a young trader who was killed there in 1828 by Comanches. Almost 200 miles from Santa Fe, the historic site is near the landmark buttes on the Santa Fe Trail, known as Rabbit Ears or Rabbit Ear Mountain. It is located almost at the center of the present border between New Mexico and Oklahoma, near Seneca, N.M.

[49] Actually dispatched the day before, the report from Lieutenant Smith reached General Kearny's camp on the Rio Grande, about 100 miles south of Santa Fe, on October 2 with official confirmation of the death of the battalion's first commander. Kearny, already on his way to California, ordered Captain Philip St. George Cooke to return to Santa Fe and take command at the rank of lieutenant colonel.

[50] Before marching on September 25, Kearny left orders at Santa Fe for the infantry battalion to move forward and "follow on our trail." To keep within supporting distance, fifty men and the best teams were picked from each company on October 3 to make a forced march to the New Mexican capital. The order stirred a rebellious mood among some of the volunteers who argued that Colonel Allen had promised Brigham Young they would be kept together in a single body.

October the 6th. On the 3d. in the afternoon we started and travailed till midnight.[51] Yesterday we travailed 25 miles. I did not get to camp till after dark, and was very tired. Today we came through two Spanish villages,[52] and the Spanish apeared very Sociable. Today we travailed between two [moun]tains, and encamped by Some Spaniards; they have everything very neat.

Wednesday Oct the 7th. Today we marched through a Spanish town[53] with music at the head, they had a Catholic Church built of mud & stone, with a cross erected [in] front. We travailed 8 or 9 miles farther and encamped. Th[ey] have milch, cheese, Apples, and green corn, to sell. [For a day] or two we have travailed through Pine, and Cedar Timber.

Thursday the 8th. I started early this morning, and [the rest] did not catch up with me till all most night. There is plenty of the balm of gilead here.

Sunday Oct the 11th. On the 9th. we marched into Santafee[54] and as we were marching through the all[e]y, the guard fired over

---

[51] The advance unit camped that night at Wagon Mound, the last great landmark on the Santa Fe Trail, near the present town of the same name in New Mexico. From this point, about twenty miles from the junction of the Cimarron Cutoff and the Mountain Branch at present Watrous, N.M., the Santa Fe Trail followed the line of today's U.S. Highway 85 over Glorieta Pass into Santa Fe.

[52] The villages of Las Vegas and Tecolote where Kearny nearly two months before had proclaimed New Mexico to be a part of the United States and administered the oath of allegiance to local citizens. At Las Vegas, the single story adobe building on which Kearny stood to issue his proclamation still overlooks the old town plaza.

[53] The town of San Miguel del Vado, or Ford of St. Michael, on the Pecos River, established about 1795 at the southernmost point on the trail which skirts the mountains to enter Santa Fe from the south.

[54] Santa Fe, officially named Villa Real de la Santa Fe de San Francisco de Asis (Royal City of the Holy Faith of St. Francis of Assisi), is one of the earliest European settlements in the western hemisphere and the oldest continuously occupied seat of government in North America. Founded between 1609 and 1614 on the Santa Fe River, it marked the high point

our heads,[55] being on a high wall. We marched on the public Square
and formed a line; we then marched to the camp ground where we
encamped.

Yesterday I washed, and cleaned my gun, and to day I and Father went to a Catholic Mass me[e]ting; they had a great many Images which [were] most beautifull; the Priest acted with great
reverence, bowing and kissing the Images, and all sorts of motions.
They also had good music. The people dispersed without much
cerimony. After the Priest had got through, I then went with Thomass
down to the store, and bought a few things necessary for comfort.

Monday the 12th. Yesterday in the afternoon there was a man
buried in soldier style.[56] Today I went with Father and Thomas down
through town to look at the place; on our rout we went to a Spanish
mill which was somewhat Singular.[57] The Spanish women gave us
some pancakes and coffee which was very good. An express came
yesterday from General Carna[58] stating that all of his men were come-

---

of Spanish expansion in the southwest and the destination of the 2,000-mile
Chihuahua Trail and the Santa Fe Trail from Missouri, nearly 800 miles
in length. The population in 1846 was about 3,000.

[55] Colonel Alexander W. Doniphan of the First Missouri Mounted
Volunteers, who then commanded American forces in New Mexico, ordered
a special salute to welcome the Mormon foot soldiers to Santa Fe. Doniphan's regiment took part in the capture of the city on August 18 without
opposition.

[56] The dead soldier probably belonged to a Missouri regiment.

[57] Of this excursion, the elder Smith wrote: "Santafe is not a large City
but it is thickly Settled the Streats [are] onely one & A half roads [rods]
wide thare gristmill was vary simple they have no bolt [to sift bran from
flour] they grind thare grain of all kinds to meal & it was vary poor at that."
See Albert Smith Journal, October 19, 1846.

[58] The Army of the West commander, whose name was often misspelled
as Carna or Kearney, had obtained a commission in 1812 to fight the British and gone on to become during nearly thirty years of service on the western frontier one of the U.S. Army's most respected field officers. In 1833,
Kearny was named lieutenant colonel of the newly formed First Dragoons
and, three years later, colonel of the mounted command which he shaped
into a crack regiment. Shortly after learning of his promotion to major
general, the New Jersey native died in 1848 from complications of yellow
fever, contracted at Vera Cruz, and the debilitating effects of wounds suffered
on December 6, 1846, in the Battle of San Pasqual.

The adobe Catholic church still stands at San Miguel del Vado, New Mexico, where Azariah Smith saw it in 1846 "with a cross erected [in] front."

ing back but one hundred which are to acompany us to [San] Francisco Bay upper California by water.[59]

Tuesday Oct the 13th. Yesterday in the afternoon the remainder of the Battalion came up except the 2nd. Co. which came up in the evening. We were glad to see them again although in a strange land. This afternoon the men that were not able to stand the journey were detaled to go by themselves a nearer rout.[60]

Thursday the 15th. Yesterday I washed my belts, and today in the forenoon I wrote a letter to mother, and in the afternoon went about town.

Friday the 16th. Last night I was detaled for guard and watched the Cattle. This forenoon the Battalion was put under guard and Searched for a Gold watch and some money, stolen from the doctor.[61]

---

[59] Kearny's decision on October 6 to leave four of his dragoon companies behind in New Mexico under Major E. V. Sumner would later prove costly. It was based on early reports that California had already been conquered by American sailors, marines, and volunteers. As Smith indicates, the general planned to move his reduced force overland to the West Coast, then go by sea to Monterey or San Francisco Bay.

[60] One of the first actions of Colonel Philip St. George Cooke, who took command this day, was to order more than a hundred members of the Mormon company, volunteers, women, and children, to join the earlier detachment at Pueblo, the small, but growing colony on the Arkansas River. The party under forty-five-year-old Captain James Brown, Company C, and First Lieutenant Elam Luddington, Company B, left Santa Fe on October 18.

[61] Other Mormon journals fail to report this robbery, but John D. Lee, not a battalion member, confirmed years later that two gold watches and some money were stolen from a trunk belonging to Battalion Surgeon Sanderson. It was Lee's opinion that Howard Egan, his partner in a secret mission to pick up the soldiers' wages, and battalion member Roswell Stevens had committed the theft and also had stolen the doctor's mules. An adopted son of Brigham Young, Lee was executed in 1877 for his role in the massacre of some 120 emigrants at Mountain Meadows, Utah Territory, in 1857. See W. W. Bishop, ed., *Mormonism Unveiled; or The Life and Confessions of the Late Mormon Bishop, John D. Lee; (Written by Himself)* (St. Louis: Bryan, Brand & Company, 1877), 187.

This afternoon we drawed two dollars & Sixty cents, from the Pay-master, and I wrote three letters for others.[62]

---

[62] Smith's father, a sergeant, said he drew $33 and "sent it to my fa-mily," but in fact all of the money paid to the soldiers was delivered to Brigham Young at Winter Quarters, the Mormon camp on the Missouri River, by the agents sent to pick up the payroll, John D. Lee and Howard Egan. Overtaking the command on the Cimarron Cutoff, the zealot Lee had raged at Lieutenant Smith and Dr. Sanderson, threatening that he would "cut your infernal throats" if they did not stop oppressing "my Brethren," or so he told his journal and later boasted to an approving Brigham Young. Since the army lacked cash to purchase even needed supplies, the battalion was paid in treasury drafts. For Lee's account of this secret assignment, see Juanita Brooks, "Diary of the Mormon Battalion Mission," *New Mex-ico Historical Review* 42, nos. 3 and 4 (1967). Also see Charles Kelly, ed., *Journals of John D. Lee, 1846–48 and 1859* (Salt Lake City: Western Printing Company, 1938), 21.

2

COOKE'S WAGON ROAD WEST
October 18, 1846–January 21, 1847

The most attractive quality of Azariah Smith was an irrepressible optimism that was shared by few of his comrades. Where others saw wasteland, Smith's eyes beheld "beautifull prairy." When his brethren complained of hardship or unfair treatment, as they often did, he would exult, "all in good health and spirits." But there had been little on the road to Santa Fe to prepare his attitude for the ordeal that lay ahead, at least as his new commanding officer saw it.

The day thirty-seven-year-old Philip St. George Cooke of the First Dragoons took command of the Mormon volunteers at Santa Fe, October 13, 1846, he almost despaired at the "extraordinary undertaking" he had been handed, even if the rank of lieutenant colonel did go with it.

It did not require twenty-one years of service in the U.S. Army, mainly on the frontier, to perceive that his new command had been "enlisted too much by families" for the mission it was expected to perform. He could easily see that "some were too old" or feeble, others "too young," and the whole outfit "embarrassed by many women." Until he got to know his men better, he also thought the untrained followers of an American prophet, who often marched to a different drummer, showed "great heedlessness and ignorance, and some obstinacy."[1]

Moreover, the assignment of the infantry battalion to march some 1,200 miles across an uncharted region and support General Kearny

---

[1] Philip St. George Cooke, *The Conquest of New Mexico and California, An Historical and Personal Narrative* (New York: G. P. Putnam's Sons, 1878), 92.

1868 photograph of the Palace of the Governors in Santa Fe much as it appeared when the Mormon Battalion camped nearby some twenty-two years before. The building still stands as a symbol of the oldest continuously occupied seat of government in North America. Photo by Nicholas Brown. Courtesy of Museum of New Mexico (neg. no. 45819).

in the conquest of California had just taken on a new dimension that added to his worry.

On the Rio Grande, Kearny and his invasion "army" of 300 dragoons, a few topographical engineers, and two brass howitzers only a week before had met the renowned scout, Kit Carson, on the way back from the Pacific Coast and learned from him such an imposing force was no longer needed. Carson bore dispatches from U.S. Navy Commodore Robert F. Stockton and Lieutenant Colonel John C. Frémont who reported, somewhat prematurely as it turned out, that they had already conquered and occupied California.

His military mission apparently accomplished, the prudent general promptly reduced his mounted force by two-thirds, an economy he would come to regret, and hurried on by packtrain to take charge of events in the far west before Stockton and Frémont got all the credit. At the same time, he directed Cooke and his Mormons to open a supply line to American forces on the Pacific Coast which meant, in effect, to make a wagon road from Santa Fe to San Diego. If it was a long way to haul supplies by wagon, the alternative was to go around Cape Horn by sea.

Handed this daunting task, Cooke was given little else that he and his command needed to carry it out—from provisions and construction tools to strong mules to haul them. To make the picture more discouraging, some anonymous bureaucrat in Washington had failed to send enough cash to the army at Santa Fe even to pay the soldiers, much less purchase supplies and livestock, assuming someone could be found to sell them.

But the tall Virginian was not a man easily turned from his duty, as his Mormon footmen were to learn, and the day he assumed military authority over them was the beginning of a historic association. Cooke was to change his mind in the months ahead as he and his men took each other's measure and found it more than sufficient to command respect, if at times grudgingly given. In the meantime, moving at once to get his five companies ready to march, he issued, on the day he took over, an order to send more than eighty sick and disabled soldiers, the laundresses and their enlisted husbands, and a number of children, more than 110 in all, to join the little Mormon colony at Fort Pueblo on the upper Arkansas River. This detachment moved out before the battalion left Santa Fe on October 19. In a further reduction, nearly sixty volunteers were ordered to go back three weeks later from a point on the Rio Grande, some 200 miles south of Santa Fe.

Even after "these two weedings," Cooke found that too many "lads and old gray-headed men still remained,"[2] acknowledging at the same time that he himself had given permission for two captains and three sergeants to take their wives along. If hardly a crack outfit in any military sense, the trimmed command was now at least a seasoned and efficient body of about 340 muskets, equal to its task.

---

[2] *Report of Lieut. Col. P. St. George Cooke of His March from Santa Fe, New Mexico to San Diego, Upper California*, Ex. Doc. 41, H. R., 30th Cong., 1st sess., 1847–48, 553.

As the expedition lost nearly a third of its complement, it was to gain in New Mexico some new members, including five worthy of note. Three were "pilots," as Smith called them, renowned mountain men, sent by General Kearny to guide the road makers around the southern reaches of the Sierra Mimbres. Pauline Weaver, a French half-breed, had trapped the Gila from its headwaters in New Mexico to its mouth at the Colorado River; Baptiste Charbonneau was the son of Sacajawea of the Lewis and Clark expedition; and early southwest trapper Antoine Leroux was the only one, Cooke noted, who didn't report to camp "more or less drunk." From this first impression, the colonel's opinion of his guides would only worsen.

But two newcomers would not only make themselves more useful, but later prove their performance was no accident. Serving as assistant quartermaster was a recent West Point honor graduate, George Stoneman, who was to become the fifteenth governor of California. And hired as interpreter was a twenty-six-year-old adventurer from New England who also helped out, when called on, as scout or assistant surgeon. Stephen Foster would go on to become the first American mayor of Los Angeles.

Thus strengthened, the command would make a wagon road to the Pacific Ocean in just 102 days, by Cooke's reckoning, a feat that seldom required the volunteers to blaze a new trail. Only on a 444-mile section, mapped by the colonel himself,[3] "From a point on Grande River to the Pimo Villages" on the Gila, north of Tucson, did the battalion actually pioneer significant sections of a new route. Even then, most of this distance, later known as Cooke's Wagon Road, followed existing Spanish or Indian trails.

At the same time, the difference between a trail and a wagon road was usually measured in untold units of hard labor and long marches without water. Some of the most difficult stretches on the entire journey were found where paths and settlements were the oldest, such as the valleys of the Rio Grande and Gila River.

In these same regions, the Mormon soldiers would see many signs that Spanish civilization in the southwest was slowly mummifying, not from the impact of a dynamic neighbor's "manifest destiny," but from the relentless bloodletting imposed by Comanche, Navaho, and Apache warriors. With Mexico City and the true Hispanic fron-

---

[3] Ibid.

tier hundreds of miles to the south, the most effective measure of conquest the Americans could bring to bear was the simple promise to protect local inhabitants from wild Indians.[4]

Before this commitment was fulfilled, portions of the road opened by the determined colonel and his men would become thoroughfares for emigrants on the southern trail to California, the San Antonio-San Diego Mail Line, and the Butterfield Overland Stage. Cooke's crude map of the stretch that took his name, later incorporated with the historic report of Kearny's topographical engineer, Lieutenant William H. Emory,[5] also would point up the importance of the Gila River's southern tributaries as corridors of transportation and commerce which, in turn, would influence the acquisition in 1854 of some 30,000 square miles that now encompass southern Arizona, including Tucson, known as the Gadsden Purchase.

Meanwhile, if young Smith was less inclined during the arduous journey ahead to marvel at the beauty of his natural surroundings, as he had often done on the trail to Santa Fe, his inborn optimism rarely flagged or failed. On the first of January 1847, over the desert sand he would rejoice: "It is now New years day and here am I going to California."

[The Journal]

Sunday Oct the 18th. Yesterday we lay in quarters eating, and [dr]inking, and last night at 9 or 10 oclock we were waked up with the News that we were to start early in the morning, and we had to draw our sticks, which was done. But today I went to another Catholic me[e]ting. They performed the same as before only the Priest delivered [a] Speach. After the me[e]ting I stayed to see the Ladies, some of which looked very prety, others looked like destruction. I then went down in town and saw a Bear, which was spry as a cat.

---

[4] For more on the decline of the Spanish frontier, see John L. Kessell, *Friars, Soldiers, and Reformers, Hispanic Arizona and the Sonora Mission Frontier, 1767-1856* (Tucson: University of Arizona Press, 1976).

[5] "Notes of a Military Reconnoisance, from Fort Leavenworth, in Missouri, to San Diego, in California," published in 1848 by the House (517-41), accompanied by the subreports of Philip St. George Cooke, A. R. Johnston, and James W. Abert.

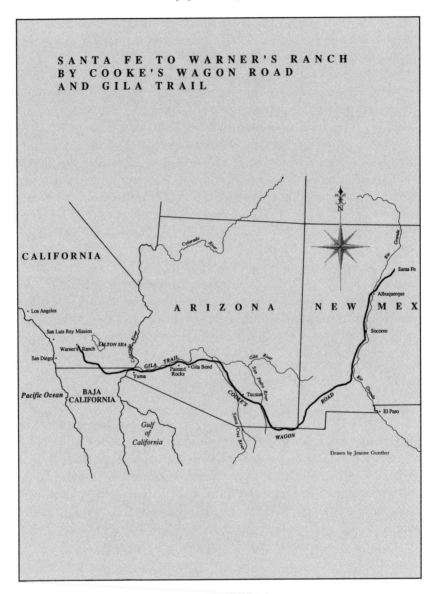

Monday Oct the 19th. This morning our former Colonel, Smith came up to see if the acount, with the Sutler was correct,[6] and about 11 oclock we left Santafee for California, under command of Colonel

---

[6] No longer acting colonel, Lieutenant Smith was carrying out the duties of his reduced assignment as commissary of subsistence.

Cook,[7] (he being apointed by General Carna, in place of J Allen) and travailed 8, or 10 miles.[8]

Tuesday the 20th. We started this morning and travailed six or eight miles when we came to a town and Springs; we travailed 4 or 5 miles farther, and camped on a Small stream which runs into the Riodelnorte. At roll call the Ajitant read orders by Colonel Cook, stating that we were to have three fourths rations of Sugar and Coffee, and two thirds rations of flour, &c till farther orders.[9]

Wednesday Oct the 21st. This morning we started and travailed 8 or 9 miles when we came to a small Stream;[10] we then travailed till after dark when we came to the Riodelnorte, it was very Sandy all the way and made it hard for the teams.

Thursday Oct the 22nd. This morning we came past another mud city, and they had Peach trees there which looked beautifull, travailing down the river Delnorte. In the afternoon [we] passed several other towns. After travailing 10 or 12 miles we encamped.

---

[7] The battalion's new commander, Philip St. George Cooke, was a native of Loudoun County, Virginia, a strict disciplinarian, and a superb field grade officer. One of the youngest cadets ever graduated from West Point, he was commissioned a second lieutenant the day after he turned nineteen. During the Civil War, he stuck with the Union and found himself outperformed at higher rank by his son, John R., and son-in-law, James Ewell Brown "Jeb" Stuart, both Confederate general officers. He retired in 1873 at the brevet rank of major general and died in 1895 at the age of eighty-five.

[8] From its camp on the outskirts of Santa Fe, the battalion the next morning began the difficult descent of the mesa shelf between Santa Fe and Albuquerque that divides New Mexico into two parts, traditionally known as Rio Arriba, "Upper River," and Rio Abajo, "Down River." For more on the route, see Peterson, Yurtinus, Atkinson, and Powell, *Mormon Battalion Trail Guide* (Salt Lake City: Utah Historical Society, 1972).

[9] Cooke attributed the reductions to shortages of supplies and the means to transport them. See Cooke's Journal, October 20, 1846.

[10] This was Galisteo Creek which the command followed to the Rio Grande where it camped on the east bank across from San Felipe Pueblo.

Friday Oct the 23d. This morning we passed a town by the name [of] Benileah,[11] where they had sweet grapes, and a great many kinds [of] fruit to Sell.

Saturday the 24th. Last night [I was] detaled for guard, and this morning started in the advance; when we came to Albikirk[12] we had to wade the river. After travailing down the river a ways we came to some of Carnas men, where we encamped.[13]

Sunday Oct the 25th. We travailed today down the river and en-camped early by a town called Lolettah[14] and in the evening we were all ca[lled] out and the Ajitant read orders concerning the mules &c.[15]

---

[11] Bernalillo, or "Little Bernal," believed named after a member of the Bernal family which resided in the area, was founded about 1695. In 1846, it was "small, but one of the best built in the territory," according to Lieu-tenant William H. Emory, head of topographical engineers for the Army of the West.

[12] Founded in 1706, Albuquerque was named in honor of the Duque de Albuquerque by New Mexico's twenty-eighth colonial governor who lo-cated the villa which would become the state's largest city "on the margins and meadows of the Rio del Norte in a goodly place of fields, waters, pasturages and timber." At this town, already as large as Santa Fe, the battalion crossed the river to follow a branch of the Chihuahua Trail on the west bank which supposedly offered a firmer road for wagons.

[13] They were Captain John Henry K. Burgwin, First Dragoons, and two of the four mounted companies that General Kearny had ordered to stay behind in New Mexico. Less than three months later, the thirty-seven-year-old North Carolinian was fatally wounded in combat against New Mex-ican insurgents at Taos where American forces under Colonel Price put down the revolt and hanged the leaders.

[14] When first discovered by the Spanish, this Indian pueblo stood on a small island in the Rio Grande, hence its true name, Isleta, or "Little Island." By 1846, shifts in the river's channel had positioned the town high and dry on the right bank.

[15] Cooke noted that he "earnestly exhorted" the Mormon company cap-tains "to lend me a more efficient assistance in requiring the mules to be properly grazed and fed, or else the expedition must very soon fall through." See Cooke's Journal, October 25, 1846.

Monday Oct the 26th. Today we passed a village where they say the Indians the day before had drove off all their Sheep and goats.[16] Today we passed over ditches which we had to jump. Some went over, lit in the water and got wet.

Tuesday Oct the 27th. There were a good many wild Geese killed today. The Spaniards have their houses nearly all covered with red peppers; they also have large droves of Goats and a good many Sheep and some hogs. Their houses are built of mud and flat roofs covered with the [word lost from torn page].

Wednesday Oct the 28th. Last night we baked bread for breacfast and dinner, and we hit the nail on the head to[o], for it [rained] and wet our chips so we could not make a fire. We travailed 8 or 9 miles and encamped in sight of mountains covered with [snow].

Thursday Oct the 29th. It was pret[t]y cold last night, and this morning we received ten catrages [cartridges] apiece, with orders that no man Should Shoot a gun, without permision from the captain, and he from the Colonel, on any occasion. For a few days back there have been a great many wild Geese killed. It was verry muddy travailing today till we came to the bend of the river where we had to push the wagons up the bluff in the Sand; after passing the bend of the river, we encamped in the timber on its banks.

Friday Oct the 30th. This morning we left the river, and went up the bluff which was verry Sandy and we had to double teams and push the wagons up. After travailing two or three miles we again came to the river and followed down till we came to a small town called Sanlorendo;[17] there was cotton growing there.

Saturday Oct the 31st. This morning I went on guard, and was on the advance, when we came to a bend in the river we had to fix

---

[16] Two shepherds had been killed and more than 10,000 sheep stolen in an audacious raid by Navaho Indians near the town of Valencia, one of the oldest Spanish settlements in the lower river region. Ibid., October 26, 1846.

[17] This may refer to San Acacia, a small agricultural settlement on the Rio Grande about sixty-five miles south of Albuquerque.

the road, and some of us had to get in the water; I saw plenty of wild geese. After passing a town called Caro[18] we encamped.

Sunday November the 1st. Last night there was a jeneral muster, and this morning, after being released from guard, and after breacfast the Battalion was called out and orders read stating that Ajitant Dikes was apointed captain [in] the place of Higgins, of Co. D.[19] and Lieutenant P. C. Merril was apointed Ajitant,[20] and at the sound of the trumpet the companies moved off and travailed twenty miles. I was verry tired and sick and could hardly get to camp.

Monday Nov. the 2nd. Today being sick I rode part of the way. Tonight there is good wood and plenty of it which is verry uncommon.

Tuesday Nov the 3d. We had a bad road today, it being very hilly and Sandy; we encamped on the banks of the river.

Wednesday Nov the 4th. Last night a man by the name of James Hampton[21] died belonging to Co. A. and this morning he was rolled

---

[18] The correct name is Socorro, or "succor," bestowed in 1598 on an Indian pueblo by the first colonizer of New Mexico, Don Juan de Onate, to commemorate the relief his expedition received after traversing the waterless stretch that became known as Jornado del Muerto, "Journey of the Dead Man."

[19] On resigning as adjutant, Dykes returned to Company D to fill the vacancy created when Captain Nelson Higgins failed to rejoin the command in time for its march from Santa Fe after escorting the first family detachment to Pueblo from the Arkansas River crossing. Higgins and his ten enlisted men were given permission to return to Pueblo.

[20] An immediate boost in morale came with the appointment of twenty-five-year-old Philemon C. Merrill, third lieutenant, Company B, as adjutant to replace the unpopular Dykes. Merrill, a New Yorker, would later become a lawman, military officer, and church leader in Utah where he died at the age of ninety-three, the father of twenty-six children by two wives.

[21] Private James Hampton, Company A, had "walked to the surgeon's but this morning," reported Cooke, but the Mormon chronicler of the command, ever ready to suggest malicious mistreatment by Dr. Sanderson, said the surgeon had pronounced him "ready for duty" when he was "far from being well." See Tyler, *Concise History*, 186.

up in his blanket and buried. Today we had a verry bad road and Thomas Woolsey,[22] one of the men that went to fort Purbelow, came up to day. He is the only one that came. He says that one of the Company was shot accidentaly on the road to Purbelow.[23]

Thursday the 5th. This morning we packed up the things ready to start; when we received orders to repitch our tents. I then cleaned my gun and went down the river. In the evening we had orders that at the beat of the drum [we] should parade; and at the playing of the music we paraded; [soon] after roll call we received orders that at any time of the night at the fireing of two guns we should repair on the ground ready for action.

Friday Nov the 6th. Today the Captain had us divided off ten to a wagon, to push them up hills and over bad places. We have only half rations now of flour and live cheafly on beaf which is very poor and tough.

Saturday Nov the 7th. We are now encamped at the place that General Carna packed his mules.[24]

---

[22] Thomas Woolsey, forty-one, a private in Company E, brought letters from family members at Pueblo. One of the escort under Captain Higgins, Woolsey apparently returned to Winter Quarters where he was chosen a member of the pioneer company under Brigham Young to enter Great Salt Lake Valley in 1847.

[23] Private Norman Sharp, Company D, also assigned under Higgins to escort families to Pueblo, accidently shot himself in the arm on the fourth day of march on the Santa Fe Trail's Mountain Branch, which would place the mishap on the left bank of the Arkansas River near the present border of Kansas and Colorado. Despite treatment by the medicine man at a "friendly Indian village," gangrene set in and Sharp died some three days later. See Tyler, *Concise History*, 165.

[24] Less than four weeks before, Kearny had camped at this spot, now under the waters of Elephant Butte Reservoir, and made the decision to turn his wagons back to Santa Fe and "pack in" to California by mules. After taking the best animals and outfits, the general left to Cooke and the Mormon Battalion "the task of opening a wagon road." See *Journal of Captain A. R. Johnston, First Dragoons*, October 9, 1846, Exec. Doc. 41, H. R., 30th Cong., 1st sess., 1847–48, 574.

Sunday Nov the 8th. Yesterday and today we had a verry bad road and had to push the wagons along; we encamped early. We have empty dishes and also bellys.

Monday Nov the 9th. Last night it was very cold, but it is warm today. This morning I was detaled for guard.

Tuesday Nov the 10th. Today 50 men of the Battalion were sent back to fort Purbelow with some teams,[25] and I wrote a letter to Mother. We packed mules and got ready to start when orders came that we would not start till tomorrow. The messes then were organized with nine in a mess.

Wednesday Nov the 11th. This morning we packed the mules, and even the oxen which packed well; we travailed about 15 miles and encamped.

Thursday Nov the 12th. This morning I was detaled to pack the mules and to [lead] a pack mule all day, and my eyes troubled me very bad.

Friday Nov the 13th. In the morning we travailed down the river a little ways when we left the river and travailed about 25 miles and encamped.[26]

---

[25] Several miles west of present Truth or Consequences, where Kearny had left the Rio Grande to head west over the mountains, Cooke at last concluded, given the condition of his men and animals, "we cannot go on so." He ordered fifty-eight of the sick and "least efficient" to return to Santa Fe under Lieutenant W. W. Willis, Company A, abandoned two heavy wagons, and lightened loads on others. See Cooke's Journal, November 9, 1846.

[26] Moving away from the Rio Grande, near present Hatch, the battalion headed southwest across an unknown region to find a wagon route to the San Pedro River, one of the Gila River's two main tributaries that flow north from Sonora, Mexico. After covering about fifteen miles (not twenty-five as Smith reports), the men camped at Foster's Hole, a rock-bound cistern in a deep ravine, named after its discoverer, the interpreter Stephen Foster. Here Cooke perched for two hours on a high ledge and oversaw the watering of mules and other animals, "cursing the men all the time." Long

Saturday Nov the 14th. This morning we baked bread for two [hours] expecting it to be thirty miles to water. At eleven oclock we started and travailed ten or twelve miles, but the Pilot[27] met us on the way and said he had found water where we would camp. We went out [of] our way a little and encamped on a small creek; there was the foundation of an ancient building there with five rooms.

Sunday Nov the 15th. This morning I was detaled for guard and stood one relief, but my ey[e]s being so sore, the orderly promised [to] detale another in my place. There was a sick ox killed today for the men but we would not eat it; some of the men went after grapes this evening.

Monday Nov the 16th. Seargeant Coray did not detale another man to stand in my place as he agreed, but Father stood in the fore, and I in the after part of the night. It snowed on [the] mountains in sight yesterday, and makes it very cold travailing; the [wind] being in the right direction. We travailed today about fifteen miles.

Tuesday Nov the 17th. This morning I got some more eye water of [the doctor] made of the rentia of silver, and we started early and travailed five hard miles, through a chain of mountains, and encamped about 11 oclock, [although] we would have had to went 25 miles around if the Pilots had [not] found this pass. Just after we had camped the Pilots [brought in] a mountain Goat which they had killed close by.

Wednesday Nov the 18th. This morning after eating our pot of Soup, (as we have not much of any thing else) Ephraim Hanks,[28] a

---

unknown, the precise location of the waterhole was recently found on Mike Hall's SS Ranch by battalion historians Carmen and Omer Smith of Arizona. See Carmen Smith, "The Lost Well of the Mormon Battalion Rediscovered," *Utah Historical Quarterly* 57 (Summer 1989): 277–86. Also see Pettegrew Journal, November 13, 1846.

[27] He was Antoine Leroux, one of the three guides ordered to pilot the Mormon force to the southern tributaries of the Gila River. Cooke thought no more of the French Canadian who joined the command near Socorro than he did of the other two guides Kearny sent to him, Pauline Weaver and Baptiste Charbonneau. Said he: "I have no guide that knows anything about the country." See Cooke's Journal, November 14, 1846.

[28] Private Ephraim Knowlton Hanks, Company B, had already served three years at sea when he joined the battalion at age nineteen. The self-reliant

man which went a hunting yesterday and layed out all night, came with a buckskin and liver, he got a mule and went after the meat but the wolves had eaten part of it. We travailed today about 20 miles when we came to the copper mine trail where we encamped.[29] I led a pack mule to day.

Friday Nov the 20th. Today we layed by hardly knowing which way to go, and the officers had a fire built on a mountain close by as a signal of distress and some Spaniards came and informed them some things concerning the rout. I bought a piece of dried beaf of them. Our rations have been raised to 10. oz. of flour and a pound and three fourths of beaf (which is very poor) to a man.

Saturday Nov the 21st. This morning we took up a line of march on the road to *Senora*; but the Colonel throught it was going to[o] far out of our ways and turned our course towards a range of mountains on our right.[30] After travailing about 12 miles we encamped haveing to go two miles after water.

Sunday Nov the 22nd. Last night we had a man up all night to see to the risings and this morning we baked bread. About 12 oclock we started and travailed twenty miles and encamped without water except what we brought with us, we made a little Soup however for supper.

Ohioan would become a noted Mormon plainsman, Indian fighter, and special agent for Brigham Young before his death at a remote mountain hideaway in southeastern Utah at age sixty-nine.

[29] This was the old Spanish road between the Santa Rita copper mines, near present Silver City, N.M., some twenty-five miles to the north, and Janos, Mexico, about 160 miles to the southeast. Known in early Spanish times, the Santa Rita pits by 1846 had become an Apache stronghold.

[30] Smith is one of the few diarists to accurately report just where Cooke was going and why he turned west after starting out on the road to Janos. Other accounts range from Henry Bigler's story that the command at first went south "for the coppermines," actually located to the north, "where we expected to meet the foe," to David Pettegrew's yarn about Cooke ordering the trumpeter to "Blow that trumpet" to the right in answer to the battalion's prayers that had gone up the night before. The colonel simply concluded the Janos road to Sonora took him too far to the south.

Philip St. George Cooke, commander of the Mormon Battalion, U.S. Army of the West, as he appeared in 1858 as lieutenant colonel of the Second Dragoons. From *Harpers Weekly*, vol. 2, no. 76, 1858, 372. Courtesy California State Library, California Section.

Monday Nov the 23d. This morning we eat our small alowance and started early and travailed about fourteen miles when we came to a range of mountains where we expected to find water but found it to be very scarce. We concluded to go to the next water which was about sixteen miles. For about three miles this side of water it was a level plain which is covered with gravel and very beautifull. I got to camp with Father about 8 oclock and found plenty of wood and water. The ox wagons with some men stayed back to the Spring all night. Our blanket wagon with some others gave out on the way. We found traiders here from which we expect to get a new recruit of mules.[31]

Tuesday Nov. the 24th. This morning brother [Laws]on came after the mules and got the blanket wagon.

Wednesday Nov the 25th. This morning we started early haveing some fresh mules, and travailed, twenty miles crossing another range of mountains,[32] which was very huge and rough, covered with timber being principally pine and oak and abounded with game. [There] was two Antilopes and a Grisly Bear killed; we encamped about sunset by the side of a small Stream haveing plenty of wood.

Thursday Nov the 26th. Today we travailed fifteen miles and there was another antilope killed in our Company.

Friday Nov the 27th. Last night I sat up till 12 oclock bakeing bread. We travailed today about fifteen miles and encamped at the foot of a mountain haveing poor wood and water. There was a great many deer and antilope Seen today and several killed, three of which were killed by the men of our Company.

Saturday Nov the 28th. This morning we travailed about seven miles, when we came to a range of mountains which we could not pass;[33] consequently we went where there was water and encamped;

---

[31] They were a party of Mexicans who refused to exchange animals, but did agree to sell twenty-one mules at an average price of about $34 each.

[32] This was the Animas range in southwestern New Mexico, last of three continental divide crossings in seven days. The Spanish name for "departed souls" was taken from a nearby settlement on the site of an ancient Indian village.

[33] One of the most difficult stretches on the march was this passage of the Guadalupe Mountains on today's border between New Mexico and Arizona. Misled by his guides, the battalion commander forced a crossing with wagons that "no other man but Cooke would ever have attempted," said Henry Bigler. Afterward, the Spanish trail passage that Cooke's guides should have known about, Guadalupe Pass, was discovered several miles to the north. See *Bigler's Chronicle*, 29.

I then went on the mountain, which was very high and could see tall mountains pileing up one above another, all covered with Small oak trees. When I arived at camp supper was ready. In the evening we baked light bread.

Sunday Nov the 29th. This morning we receaved orders that the mules should be packed and four men from each mess, to go with them, nine miles over the pass, and then return, considring it to be the most convenient pass found by the pilots, which returned last night with an Indian chief.[34]

Monday Nov the 30th. Last evening [the] men returned with the mules, and this morning we packed up [and] Started, passing the back bone of America, from the waters of the Atlantic, to the waters of the Pacific Ocean.[35] I led a pack mule. Some of the wagons got broke comeing down a very bad mountain, b[ig] and almost perpendicular. I and Father brother Rogers and Law[son][36] is now in a mess by ourselves.

Tuesday December the 1st. This morning we again loaded the wagons and travailed Five miles and encamped.

Wednesday Dec the 2nd. This morning we started early and travailed about seven miles and encamped by [a] forsaken city[37] and

---

[34] He was the wary Apache, Manuelita, whose friendship Cooke courted in the hope of obtaining fresh mules. Five days earlier, the colonel had sent Leroux and a newly hired Mexican guide ahead to scout the trail to the San Bernardino ranch, find the Apaches, and bring them to him. See Cooke's Journal, November 29, 1846.

[35] While the Guadalupe Mountains severely tested men and animals, the range did not mark the continental divide, already passed for the last time some days before.

[36] Samuel Rogers, twenty-seven, and John Lawson were both privates in Smith's company. Rogers later became a bishop in southern Utah while Lawson, like the Smiths, settled in Sanpete County.

[37] The abandoned San Bernardino Hacienda had served as headquarters of a ranch established in 1822 by one Lieutenant Ignacio Perez on a 73,240-acre grant from the Mexican government. Perez had justified his request for so much land on the claim it would be a buffer against the

a good many Indians came to traid, they [were] verry sociable, but probably on acount of our superior numbers. One man got lost and fell in with Some of them, they stript [him] of his arms, and ammonition to do the best he could, and fortunately he found camp the next day.[38] The Indians have plenty of [baked roots] to sell but they will take buttons sooner than money.

Thursday Dec the 3d. We layed by today and I washed some Cloth[e]s. There was several wild cattle killed today which are tender and g[ood].[39]

Friday Dec the 4th. This morning we had four days rations [of] beaf dealt out to us, and at one oclock we started and travailed [8] miles and encamped between two mountains, haveing good [wood] and water.

Saturday Dec the 5th. Last [night] we jerked our beaf and started early this morning and travailed about sixteen miles and encamped on a plain.[40] There was several wild cattle killed today.

Apaches, but by 1846 the natives had taken over the ranch and made it into their own hunting ground for up to 100,000 wild cattle from the abandoned spread and a similar venture on the San Pedro River. Before that, the fine San Bernardino spring, now located just south of the line between Cochise County, Arizona, and Mexico, had served for more than a century as a favorite camping place on the road, followed for some miles by the battalion, between Janos and Fronteras.

[38] Private John Allen, Company E, apparently tried to desert, but the encounter with Apaches made him glad to get back to the command with his whole skin. Identified by some as the only non-Mormon volunteer, this miscreant apparently joined the faith just to qualify for the march to California at government expense. He was later excommunicated for misconduct. See Tyler, *Concise History*, 213; *Bigler's Chronicle*, 30; and Cooke's Journal, December 3, 1846.

[39] Enough wild bulls were killed to supply fresh meat to the entire command for about two weeks.

[40] The battalion camped at a spring, just across the border from present Douglas, Ariz., so overrun by wild livestock that Cooke thought it a "perfect cattleyard in appearance." See Cooke's Journal, December 5, 1846.

Sunday Dec the 6th. We travailed about sixteen miles and encamped at a grove haveing good water. It is very cold and snowed a little this evening.

Monday Dec. the 7th. This morning there was men dispatched with mules after the meat that was killed yesterday and in the afternoon they arived with the beaf.

Tuesday Dec the 8th. This morning brother Elisha Smith[41] died belonging to Co. E. We travailed about twenty miles and encamped haveing no water only what we brought with us.

Wednesday Dec the 9th. We started early this morning and travailed about ten miles when we came to a small stream called San Pedro. After watering our teams we went down San Pedro about six miles and encamped.[42]

Thursday Dec the 10th. We travailed today about fourteen miles down the river haveing a good road and this evening I went a fishing and caught two fine Salmon. Father and brother Lawson went about three miles after beaf some of the men haveing killed a wild Bull today.

Friday Dec. the 11th. We travailed twelve miles. On the way three men was run over by wild Bulls, one of them was Father and hurt him very much. There was also two mules killed by them.[43]

---

[41] Not a regular member of the battalion, forty-eight-year-old Elisha Smith had been hired as a teamster and servant by his friend, Captain Daniel Davis of Company E. Before the unit marched, he was buried on the bank of a "beautiful little stream of water running through an ash grove," according to Henry Bigler. See *Bigler's Chronicle*, 31.

[42] The San Pedro River, which flows north into the Gila River, was probably the stream referred to as "Rio Nexpa" by Francisco Vasquez de Coronado in 1540 when his expedition moved down the waterway in search of the fabled Seven Cities of Cibola. For the next fifty miles or so the battalion would literally march in the tracks made by the famous Spanish explorer more than three centuries before.

[43] Wild bulls along the San Pedro River finally struck back at their tormentors when a number of wounded animals ran up from the river bottom and found some battalion members "in the way of thare retreat." The frenzied animals injured several soldiers, including Albert Smith who reported

San Pedro River in southern Arizona at the place where Mormon soldiers fought wild bulls on Coronado's trail.

Saturday Dec. the 12th. We travailed today fifteen miles and en-camped on the banks of the river. There was more beaf killed today than we could make use of.

Sunday Dec. the 13th. Today we travailed eight miles in the fore-noon and in the afternoon mustered, but was somewhat awkward which made the Colonel swear very much. After the parade he read orders stating that under existing circumstances we would go through a small mexican gar[r]ison called Tubson.[44]

Monday Dec. the 14th. This morning I was detaled on guard and travailed twenty two miles.

Tuesday Dec. the 15th. In the morning we passed a still, and they had corn and meal to Sell. Three Mexican soldiers were taken prisoners today Supposed to be Spies.[45] Today we travailed fifteen miles.

Wednesday Dec the 16th. This morning mr Foster,[46] one of the Pilots which the mexicans had taken prisoner was released, and we

---

"one chased me & as he came up threue me & run over me & tho there was no bones broke yet I was hurt vary Seriously." See Albert Smith Journal, December 11, 1846.

[44] After some drills on loading and firing and instruction on how to form a line from a column, Cooke ordered an advance on Tucson, a "garrisoned town," explaining "any other course is a hundred miles out of the way." The command now left the San Pedro River at the present town of Benson, Ariz., and headed on the line of present Interstate 10 for the walled presi-dio on the Santa Cruz River, nearly fifty miles away, ready to offer battle. See Orders No. 19, Headquarters Mormon Battalion, Cooke's Journal, De-cember 13, 1846.

[45] Near a waterhole, where some Mexicans and Indians were making mescal whiskey, Cooke took four Mexican dragoons prisoner to guarantee the safety of Foster, his fearless interpreter, who had gone ahead into Tuc-son where he had been promptly disarmed and put under guard. The colo-nel sent one of the captive dragoons to the town with a note offering to free the other three on Foster's prompt release. Ibid., December 15, 1846.

[46] Born in Maine, Foster had graduated from Yale, taught school in Virginia, studied medicine in Louisiana, and sought his fortune as a trader in New Mexico before he joined Cooke at Santa Fe at age twenty-six. Later,

Mission San Xavier del Bac, the "White Dove of the Desert," now restored, had been ransacked by marauding Apaches long before Cooke's command occupied nearby Tucson, founded in 1776 to protect Spanish locations in the Santa Cruz Valley.

also released ours. We started early and when we got to Tubson the Soldiers had all left and had also forced [out] part of the inhabitants without giveing them time to remove much of their property, and left their houses without inhabi[tants].[47]

The Colonel has taken all of the public property that he can find and started the mills grinding wheat. This evening we bought some flour and beans.

Thursday Dec. the 17th. Today we layed by and fed on wheat. We bought some more beans today and eat our fill once more.

Friday Dec the 18th. Last night about twelve oclock there was an alarm, and in five minits the whole Battalion was in arms; Company A. Marched to town to see what was up, and we formed across the road ready for battle. In about a half an hour Company A. came back without seeing a single man.[48] We then was dismissed till morning when we started and travailed 28 miles on a level barren plain, and encamped about ten oclock, and fed the mules on wheat brought along for the purpose.[49]

---

in California, he once resigned temporarily his office as mayor of Los Angeles to join a lynch mob and dispense vigilante justice to a convicted murderer. After years of public service, he died in Los Angeles at age seventy-eight.

[47] Rather than fight or accept Cooke's bid for a token surrender, the garrison of about 130 men with two brass cannons had abandoned the town. When the Americans marched in, Tucson was a fortified settlement, or presidio, of about 500 inhabitants, mostly soldiers and their families. Founded in 1776 to protect the nearby Mission San Xavier del Bac and other Spanish locations in the Santa Cruz Valley, the town by 1846 was virtually isolated by the Apaches and in disrepair from neglect by the Mexican government.

[48] A nervous picket guard had reported falsely that a Mexican army was coming.

[49] The command would now follow the historic Gila River route to southern California, first opened in 1774 by Padre Francisco Tomás Hermenegildo Garcés, Franciscan missionary and founder of Tucson, and the Spanish colonizer, Juan Bautista de Anza, who then commanded the presidio at Tubac, some forty-seven miles south of Tucson. The following year, Colonel Anza led an expedition of 240 men, women, and children over this

Saturday Dec the 19th. Started early and I travailed about twenty miles when I came where the rear guard had stoped, and I was so lame that I could hardly move. I layed by the fire and rested till about four oclock in the morning, and then went eight miles to camp.

Sunday Dec the 20th. When I got to camp they had just started. We travailed about eighteen miles and encamped by water standing in ponds on the ground.

Monday Dec the 21st. Last night I stood guard and today travailed eighteen miles and encamped on the Ahelia River.⁵⁰ This evening more than two hundred Indians came to camp to traid and we bought more beans.

Tuesday Dec the 22nd. We travailed 10 miles and en[camped] by an indian village on the river, and the indians came in camp [by the] hundreds, and nearly every Squaw had a child in her arms.⁵¹

Wednesday Dec the 23d. We travailed about twenty on[e miles] and passed several small indian villages consisting of small huts [with fires] in the centre.

---

trail to San Gabriel Mission, near Los Angeles, thence north to San Francisco Bay where he founded in 1776 the presidio and mission that became San Francisco. The Gila River and its tributaries later formed one of the three main corridors of western expansion.

⁵⁰ The command reached the Gila River and found General Kearny's trail, now about six weeks old, near the present town of Sacaton on the Gila River Indian Reservation. Here Cooke completed an excellent map, made with little more than a compass, of the looping, 444-mile track from the Rio Grande to the Gila River, later known as Cooke's Wagon Road, included with his report. See *Report of Lieut. Col. P. St. George Cooke* (referred to hereafter as Cooke's Report).

⁵¹ The Pima Indian villages were scattered along both sides of the Gila River some twenty miles, according to Albert Smith. Peaceful in their relations with Americans, the Pimas were described by Cooke as a "friendly, guileless and singularly innocent and cheerful people." See Cooke's Report, 557.

Thursday Dec the 24th. Today we layed by [and I and] Father washed. Today the camp was crouded with indians and a good [many things] was stolen by them.[52]

Friday Dec the 25th. We started [at] eleven oclock and travailed eighteen miles and encamped about eight [oclock] in the evening without water.

Saturday Dec the 26th. I was one of the front guard, and arived at the river about Sundown. The wagons did not get to camp till in the night.

Sunday Dec the 27th. We travailed ten miles and encamped by [good] grass for our teams which is very uncommon.

Monday Dec the 28th. We travailed about ten miles [and encamped] about a mile from the river.

Tuesday [Dec the 29th.] We left the river today and travailed in a westerly direction. [We] passed a pile of huge rocks covered with engravings pecked on the rocks in all shapes and forms.[53]

Wednesday Dec the 30th. Today we travailed twenty miles, and had several bad hills and had to pull the wagons up by means of ropes.

Thursday Dec the 31st. We travailed today about ten miles haveing a very good road.

---

[52] This camp was at Maricopa Wells, about eight miles north of today's town of Maricopa, the last watering place before the trail cut across a loop of the Gila River on a dry stretch of some forty miles before returning to the river at present Gila Bend. Maricopa Wells was later a station on the San Antonio and San Diego mail route and the Butterfield Overland Stage Line.

[53] Increasingly defaced by vandals, these petroglyphs of animals, men, and mystic figures can be seen today at Painted Rocks Historic State Park, located about fourteen miles west of Gila Bend, Ariz., between Interstate 8 and the river. The rock pile covers less than an acre and possibly marks a prehistoric boundary between Indian tribes.

Painted Rocks, ancient Indian petroglyphs on the Mormon Battalion's route
along the Gila River, that appear to define a prehistoric boundary between
tribes.

Friday January 1st. 1847. We started early this morning and travailed about ten miles down the river and encamped on its banks. This evening we have taken two wagon boxes being made tight for the purpose and put them in the river, to take a load down in them.[54] It is now new Years day and here am I going to California.

Saturday Jan. 2nd. When we arived here last evening we found two families, one Scotch and the other English encamped here; the men can talk good english, and are intelligent good looking people.[55] A great many mules were lost last night and we did not start till late and travailed twelve miles I being on guard.

Sunday Jan the 3d. Last night I stood guard, and started early this morning and travailed about twelve miles. Today the old guard was all put on extra duty on acount of their being so many mules lost the night before.

Monday Jan the 4th Haveing left one of our wagons I and Father have to sleep out doors, So I crawl in a Buffalo sack, and sleep as warm as a pig, although it is very cold. We travailed today eight or ten miles. We have sent men with pack mules back to find the

---

[54] To ease the load on his tired mules, Cooke attempted to float more than a ton of provisions and luggage down river on a raft made by lashing two wagon boxes together, end to end, between two cottonwood logs. The experiment failed because the stream was too shallow, even then, to carry the loaded vessel over sandbars. Water usage upstream now makes this stretch of the river normally dry.

[55] One of these families belonged to an American, William Money, whose Mexican wife had delivered a baby two days before and ridden ten miles on horseback the day after. Money in 1837 had gone to Sonora where his Protestant religious views had made him unwelcome in the mission vista of San Antonio de Oquitoa. The Moneys were on their way from California to a mining town near the present Arizona border where her father lived when they had been reduced to eating horse flesh. See Cooke's Journal, December 27, 28, 1846–January 3, 1847; John L. Kessell, *Friars, Soldiers, and Reformers: Hispanic Arizona and the Sonora Mission Frontier, 1767–1856* (Tucson: University of Arizona Press, 1976), 304.

wagon boxes, but have heard nothing from them yet.[56] This evening I and Father climb a very high mountain with several others and rolled down rocks.

Tuesday Jan the 5th. We travailed today about twelve miles and encamped, after which our rations were reduced to nine oz. of flour, and a half pound of pork pr man, as we have but very little provision to last us through to settlements about fourteen days travail.

Wednesday Jan the 6th. We travailed fifteen miles, and this evening a wagon box arived[57] at camp haveing left very near all of the provision.

Thursday Jan the 7th. We travailed today about thirteen miles.

Friday Jan the 8th. We travailed about eighteen miles and encamped at the mouth of the Ahelia about a mile from the Cholerado.[58]

Saturday Jan the 9th. Last night we had all the sugar and coffee dealt out to us being 6t [sic] oz of sugar and 4 oz of coffee to the man. We started early this morning and travailed twelve miles when we came to the Cholerado where we are a going to cross.[59] This evening

---

[56] Corporal William S. Muir, a twenty-four-year-old Scottish convert to Mormonism, and five men from Company A were sent back with pack mules to recover at least a portion of the flour from the ill-fated attempt to float provisions down the Gila River on an improvised raft. See Cooke's Journal, January 4, 5, 1847; Golder, *Standage*, 201.

[57] The watertight wagon boxes, built to serve as boats or pontoons when needed, were floated empty downstream and later used to ferry baggage and provisions across the Colorado River.

[58] Near the eastern outskirts of present Yuma, Ariz. On receiving the waters of its Gila tributary, the Colorado River flowed due west for about ten miles before turning south to go into the Gulf of California.

[59] The battalion camped on the east bank of the Colorado River, opposite the present town of Algodones, Mexico, where three of the party sent to recover flour returned with more than 400 pounds. They reported Corporal Muir and two others had gone to look for more, but would return in two days. After a heroic effort, they rejoined the command in California more than two weeks later with another 400 pounds.

the teamsters with others gathe[red] Muskeet for the mules which they will eat as well as oats.

Sunday Jan the 10th. We layed by today and I and Father gather[ed] some muskeet and ground it in a coffee mill, to help our half rations. Muskeet grows on small trees, and when ground looks like meal, being somewhat sweat [sweet]. Several pack mules came up loaded with provision which was left back on the river. This afternoon some of the battalion crossed the river.[60]

Monday Jan the 11th. This morning the rest of the Battalion crossed the river; I with a good many others rode a mule as it would take to[o] long to take all across in the boat. Several mules fell down in the water and drowned. After crossing the river we travailed fifteen [miles] and obtain[ed] water by diging.[61] The sheep and a good many men have not arived at Camp.

Tuesday Jan the 12th. We travailed about twelve miles and I drove a pack mule haveing left another wagon (and have only one public wagon in the company,) we encamped without water on a plain.

---

[60] Its bed as much as a mile wide and several channels hundreds of yards across, the muddy Colorado River presented a formidable barrier that claimed several mules in its swift current and took two days to cross near Pilot Knob. Ahead lay an even greater challenge—the Colorado Desert.

[61] Smith's entry fails to convey the anxiety felt by the battalion's commander at this unknown desert location, now inside Mexico, where his exhausted soldiers found a dead wolf in the dry well, and when they dug deeper for water, struck quicksand that caved in before a puddle could form. For Cooke, it was "the most trying hour of my long military service." The day was saved by a washtub, hauled all the way from Nauvoo by Susan Davis who refused to surrender it voluntarily even if the lives of all did depend on it. The tub was taken from her, the bottom knocked out and placed in the well to keep the sides from collapsing. As the hole was deepened, "a radiant glow of light" came over the colonel when enough water flowed to "be dipped with a camp kettle," he recorded in his journal, January 11, 1847, and later Report, 558. Susan and Daniel Davis later settled in Farmington, Utah, in the county that took the captain's name. But when he died in 1850 near Fort Kearny, while the couple was traveling east on business, the defiant Susan just kept going and never came west again.

Wednesday Jan the 13th. We travailed ten miles when we came to water being in wells from twelve to fifteen foot deep.[62]

Thursday Jan the 14th. This morning we buried some hav[ersacks] a broken gun and some amonition. The company also sold their mules and left the wagon. We started about twelve oclock and trav[ailed] twenty miles and encamped about nine in the evening without wa[ter].

Friday Jan the 15th. We started early this morning and travailed ten miles when we met some indians with a pilot which came from General Carna haveing some fresh mules and ten head of beaf ca[ttle]. They also brought news that Carna had had a battle, haveing twen[ty] men killed and only one of the oposite party injured.[63] I help gua[rd] the mules, which was very wild, while the Indians caught them with lassoes made for the purpose; after chokeing them till they were weak they would trip them up and catch them. After eating a little dinner we travailed sixteen miles and encamped about eight oclock.

---

[62] Known to history as the Alamo Mocha Well, this campsite was about six miles south of today's border between Mexico and Imperial County, California. Of the Imperial Valley crossing, Albert Smith said: "Some went A head with [pick] & Shovel in hand & dug wel[l]s in low places So that we did not quite parish."

[63] The price for Kearny's decision to leave most of his dragoon companies in New Mexico was paid on December 6 when his reduced command encountered a larger body of mounted lancers on the trail to San Diego. When the dragoons on trail-worn mules foolishly charged, their opponents, splendid horsemen from southern California ranches, retreated until the headlong rush was spent, then wheeled and cut the winded attackers to pieces with long willow lances. The unequal fight, sabers against lances, lasted not much longer than fifteen minutes, but in that time twenty-one Americans were killed, including three of the most promising officers of the First Dragoons, and almost as many wounded, including Kearny himself, about one-third of his force. Virtually unscathed, the Californians also rode off with one of the brass howitzers the dragoons had hauled all the way from Fort Leavenworth, an embarrassing loss. The site of this action, bloodiest in the military occupation of California, is now marked by the San Pasqual Battlefield State Historical Monument, located some seven miles east of Escondido on State Highway 78.

The ruins of Warner's Ranch in San Diego County today mark the location of the first California settlement on the southern overland route to the Pacific shore.

Saturday Jan the 16th. We started about two in the morning and travailed twenty miles, without any water when we came to spring very much fatagued.[64] Brother Lawson left his mule, pack and all; after resting he went back after it, but did not find it.

---

[64] The command completed without water a march of nearly sixty miles in forty-eight hours to cover the worst stretch of desert and arrive at Carrizo Creek, a stream of intermittent flow on the Southern Emigrant Trail.

Sunday Jan the 17th. We travailed ten miles haveing a [bad] sandy road.

Monday Jan the 18th. We layed by and washed, and in the afternoon had a parade.

Tuesday Jan the 19th. Our flour and pork haveing all [gone] we have nothing but beaf and not enough of that.

The companies went ahead of the wagons today, and we went through a pass that was so narrow that we had to chop the rocks away with axes. We encamped without water haveing travailed about eight miles.

Wednesday Jan the 20th. We travailed seven miles before breacfast after we travailed six miles farther.

Thursday Jan the 21st. We travailed about fifteen miles when we came to Warners Settlement where we encamped.[65]

---

[65] After marching 1,125 miles from Santa Fe, by Cooke's estimate, Smith and his comrades arrived at the settlement that was to travelers on the Southern Overland Trail what Johnson's Ranch and Sutter's Fort were to immigrants on the more heavily traveled road along the Humboldt River, a haven at the California end of the trail. The 49,000-acre Warner's Ranch was owned by Jonathan Trumbull Warner, known in California as John J. Warner, a native of Connecticut who had headed west at age twenty-four and worked for Jedediah S. Smith in 1831 when the renowned fur trader and explorer was killed by Comanches on the Cimarron Cutoff. From New Mexico, he went on to California where he changed his name to Juan José Warner, took out Mexican citizenship, and became one of the largest landholders. Among the earliest to advocate American annexation of California, Warner served as a confidential agent of Thomas Larkin, American consul at Monterey, and supported the American side during the occupation. Despite this record, he was arrested briefly at San Diego on suspicion of disloyalty during the Stockton conquest. A founder and first president of the Historical Society of Southern California, he died at Los Angeles in 1895. The ruins of Warner's ranch buildings can be seen today on San Diego County Road S2 less than a mile from its junction with State Highway 79, about 13.5 miles north of Santa Ysabel.

3

CALIFORNIA OCCUPIED
January 22–July 20, 1847

After marching steadily for five months and 2,000 miles, often on short rations and little water, Azariah Smith would now find a time of relative abundance and tranquility. Yet with garrison duty would come a longing to see his mother and a sickness of the spirit for a place few of his people knew in the first months of 1847, a place they could call home.

The Mormon youngster and his comrades arrived in California too late to take part in the final battles of the conquest, only two weeks before, around Los Angeles. But they came just in time to become a counter in a remarkable, and potentially dangerous, confrontation between American military leaders over who was in charge in the newly occupied province.

General Kearny's claim to such authority rested on written orders from the secretary of war in June 1846, to "press forward" after occupying New Mexico and take "earliest possession of Upper California." To encourage Kearny, then a colonel, to get on with the task, the secretary said that President Polk himself promised that "the rank of brevet brigadier general will be conferred on you as soon as you commence your movement" from Santa Fe "towards California."

Should he occupy both New Mexico and California, "or considerable places in either," Kearny's orders authorized him to "establish civil governments," cautioning that he always "act in such manner as best to conciliate the inhabitants."[1] The general's duty was clear;

---

[1] W. L. Marcy to S. W. Kearny, June 3, 1846, in Exec. Doc. 60, H. R., 30th Cong., 1st sess., 1847–48, 153–55.

he was not the sort to surrender it lightly; however, a couple of countrymen more colorful than he had gotten there first.

When Commodore Robert Field Stockton took command of the Pacific Squadron in July 1846, the U.S. Navy had already occupied Monterey and San Francisco, and stood ready to support an occupation of California by land. But the grandson of a Declaration of Independence signer, eager to launch a political career, saw his opportunity for fame and moved at once to make the most of it.

Occupying Los Angeles and San Diego, Stockton shortly announced that in less than a month he had put the ''Mexican army'' to flight, restored peace and harmony, and established a new civil government.[2] The commodore also proclaimed himself by right of conquest supreme commander and governor, titles he later bestowed on his subordinate in these exploits, Lieutenant Colonel John C. Frémont of the topographical engineers.

No shrinking violet himself when it came to glory seeking, the thirty-nine-year-old ''Pathfinder'' had come west to explore and stayed on the coast to lead the American filibusters who proclaimed California a republic under the Bear Flag and fought to add it to the United States. Commanding the irregular California Battalion, Frémont had supported Stockton when it suited him, but seemed at times only to serve a vision of himself as leader of a new nation on the western shore.[3]

If Kearny appeared outclassed by such men, the dragoon soldier finally got his chance because the wisdom ''to conciliate'' the conquered, set forth in his own orders, was not to be found in his ambitious navy opponent. Less than six weeks old was the commodore's infant government when Californians in the south, stung by bombast and arbitrary decrees, overthrew it and recovered most of the region, including Los Angeles.

With only a few dozen men of his own left, Kearny made peace with Stockton long enough to defeat the insurgents with a combined American force as he awaited the arrival of Cooke and his Mormon infantry. In a region of fewer than 15,000 inhabitants, Spanish and

---

[2] R. F. Stockton to G. Bancroft, August 28, 1846, in Exec. Doc. 4, H. R., 29th cong., 2nd sess., Dec. 8, 1846.

[3] For Frémont's role in the California conquest and aftermath, see Donald Jackson and Mary Lee Spence, eds., *The Expeditions of John Charles Frémont*, vol. 2 of 3 (Urbana: University of Illinois Press, 1970).

Americans, some 330 muskets, strategically placed at San Luis Rey Mission, would then add weight to the general's assertion of the authority that was lawfully his, while the contending parties awaited word from Washington, a line of communication that usually took at least three months to clear, one way.

In the meantime, the Mormon Battalion's colonel, whose sense of humor had somehow survived every trial, found himself commanding the only "legal force in California," at the same rank as Frémont, yet the only one "not pretending to the highest authority of any sort."

"General Kearny is supreme—somewhere up the coast; Colonel Frémont supreme at Pueblo de los Angeles; Commodore Stockton is Commander-in-chief at San Diego," he portrayed the almost comical standoff, "and we are all supremely poor; the government having no money and no credit; and we hold the Territory because Mexico is poorest of all."[4]

The only course Cooke could take under the circumstances was to prepare his men for whatever might come, which meant for Smith and his comrades drill and more drill.[5] At the same time, most of them counted the days until their twelve-month enlistments expired and prepared to rejoin their families, somewhere to the east.

During the months ahead, the Mormon soldiers would see a land unlike any other they had known and bid farewell to Philip St. George Cooke, a professional soldier they had learned to respect, some even to admire. And young Smith would suffer an injury that would later darken the early years of his adult life with an affliction no one in those days understood.

For Azariah Smith, it would be a lonesome time, spent far from his loved ones, "my dear Mother and Sisters." Often would he yearn to see them as he would long for a home in "Zions city, most glorious to behold," the New Jerusalem his people would someday build, "Whose walls are made of jasper and streets of purest Gold."

---

[4] Philip St. George Cooke, *The Conquest of New Mexico and California, An Historical and Personal Narrative* (New York: G. P. Putnam's Sons, 1878), 289.

[5] For the most recent history of the California occupation, see Neal Harlow, *California Conquered, War and Peace on the Pacific 1846–1850* (Berkeley: University of California Press, 1982).

[The Journal]

Friday Jan the 22nd. This morning after breacfast I and Father went up to see the folks but could not get any thing to eat. There is a spring here so hot that I could not bear my hand in it.

Saturday Jan. the 23d. Haveing receaved a fresh supply of beaf cattle, we draw four pound of beaf to the man. We travailed today twenty miles and encamped about dusk.

Sunday Jan. the 24th. Last night it rained and we got some wet, but today we travailed four miles, raining the most of the time but the clouds passed off and looked pleasant in the evening.

Monday Jan the 25th. We travailed sixteen miles when we came to an Indian camp, and the Indians were in a line of battle. We encamped about half a mile from them and used a carell [corral] for wood. The Indians were burying their dead which had been killed in a battle with the Spaniards.[6]

Tuesday Jan. the 26th. We travailed sixteen miles and had a good road. We crossed a creek which we had to waid and then encamped. Haveing received an express from Carna we are on our way to Sandiego.[7]

Wednesday Jan the 27th. We travailed twenty miles and came in sight of the Pacific Ocean. The hills and plains are green and look

---

[6] These were the Luiseño, or Temecula, Indians who had lost some thirty-eight killed in an ambush some days before by Californians and their Cahuilla tribe allies. The Luiseños took their name from the San Luis Rey Mission, located in their territory. They were friendly toward the battalion because Cooke had hired a chief and twenty warriors to drive cattle and act as scouts. See Cooke's Journal, January 21, 1847. Also see Horace Parker, "The Temecula Massacre," *The Westerners Brand Book*, Los Angeles Corral, Book ten, 1963.

[7] After starting out to bring the battalion into action in support of Kearny's advance on Los Angeles, Cooke received word the town was occupied and the general already on his way back to San Diego. With hostilities ended, Cooke headed the command for the latter place as originally ordered.

San Luis Rey de Francia as pictured before the arrival of the Mormon Battalion to occupy the "king" of Spanish missions in California. Courtesy of California State Library, California Section.

most beautifull. We passed Sanlouis Ray, where there was a Catholic Church, about four miles from the ocean, but the inhabitants have all left.[8]

Thursday Jan the 28th. We travailed about eighteen miles. We have a large drove of beef cattle which we have gathered up on the road, which are very good.

---

[8] San Luis Rey de Francia, the "king" of California's missions and largest in the Americas, had been systematically plundered by government administrators and abandoned under the 1833 law that secularized the California missions, reducing them to a "pitiful state" within six years. Named after Louis IX, king of France, the mission when dedicated in 1798 brought to eighteen the number that formed a chain, one day's travel apart, from San Diego to San Francisco Bay. Now restored, this magnificent mission is located four miles east of Interstate 5 on Mission Avenue in Oceanside. For the Mexican law to "extinguish" the California missions, and subsequent decrees, see Sen. Doc. 18, 31st Cong., 1st sess., 1849–50, vol. 9, 149–68.

Friday Jan. the 29th. We travailed eighteen miles when we came to old Sandiego where we expected to quarter, about nine miles from the Coast.[9]

Saturday Jan. the 30th. Today was spent at washing mending and all sorts of business. And this evening a company of dragoons, being some of Carnas men came here.

Sunday Jan the 31st. The dragoons say they have had four battles, and twenty men and upwards killed.[10]

Monday Febuary the 1st. Receiving orders from head quarters we started, with the Dragoons, on our way back to San louis Ray to take up our quarters there;[11] we travailed sixteen miles and encamped.

Tuesday Feb. the 2nd. We travailed twenty miles.

Wednesday Feb. the 3d. We travailed twelve miles when we came to Sanlouis Ray, I being on guard.

---

[9] The battalion camped near Mission San Diego de Alcalá, the mother of Alta California's Spanish missions, then an abandoned shell, "dilapidated and full of Indians and dirt," according to Cooke. Dedicated in 1760 by the renowned Franciscan Father Junípero Serra and moved five years later to its present location, six miles up the San Diego River, the mission in its glory days counted nearly 1,500 Christian Indians and included a school, vineyards, gardens, and grazing lands. It has also been restored.

[10] The two companies of First Dragoons that came to California with General Kearny, numbering a few more than 100 officers and men, suffered nineteen killed or mortally wounded, all but two by lances, at the Battle of San Pasqual on December 6, 1846, and at least one killed and possibly others who died later of wounds suffered during the so-called "battles" of San Gabriel on January 8 and Los Angeles on January 9, 1847.

[11] The more strategic location at San Luis Rey placed the battalion between Los Angeles and San Diego where it could move on short notice against insurrections at either point as well as confront an enemy incursion from Sonora. It also positioned the force to move against Frémont at Los Angeles in the event he continued to defy Kearny's authority. Frémont at the time considered himself governor and military commander of California.

Thursday Feb the 4th. Last night I stood guard, and this morning, after being discharged, I went up to quarters and there is a police detaled to clean the Square, which is well finished and looks nice.[12] This evening the ajitant read orders concerning the travail and labour of the Mormon Battalion which was well Suited out.[13]

Friday Feb the 5th. This afternoon the orderly read an order that all the private mules and horses were to be disposed of by the fifteen[th] of this month.

Saturday Feb the 6th. We washed our belts and prepared for a jeneral inspection tomorrow.

Sunday Feb the 7th. This morning after breacfast we were called out and both ourselves and quarters inspected; and this evening the Company was divided into Squads and are to drill every day.[14]

Monday Feb. the 8th. We was drilled without our arms today, and it is the first time that I ever was taught how to turn around.

---

[12] David Pettegrew found San Luis Rey Mission "pleasantly situated" with a "church in the southeast corner built square and on the front or south side is a row of pillars that supports an arch on which was a walk that went around the building." To Albert Smith, it was a "butiful place it is built like A fort . . . in the Southeast Corner of the fort thare is a larg[e] Chapple with 6 bells & any Amount of [images]."

[13] Cooke's famous Order No. 1, in which battalion members justly took pride, was dated January 30 at San Diego, but not read before the command until roll call on February 4 at San Luis Rey Mission. Among other commendations, he said, "History may be searched in vain for an equal march of infantry." Never one to hide his own light, the colonel was quite aware that his somewhat exaggerated praise also reflected favorably on himself.

[14] With garrison duty came the long-delayed military instruction that would qualify many battalion members to become leaders of the territorial militia, or Nauvoo Legion, in Utah. Two months later, Kearny's successor, Colonel Richard B. Mason, First Dragoons, saw the Mormon soldiers "go through the manual and firings" and reported they "acquitted themselves with a good deal of credit." See Sen. Doc. 18, 31st Cong., 1st sess., 1849–50, vol. 9, 272.

Tuesday Feb. the 9th. We had orders to return all our catrages [cartridges] by ten.

Wednesday Feb. the 10th. This afternoon I and Father ground some Corn that we got of the indians, and had a fine supper.

Thursday Feb. the 11th. After breacfast Father, Thomas and myself [got] permision of the captain to take a walk down to the Pacific, about four miles; when we got there the Ocean was all in a foam. I saw a very large Whale bone on the coast. I have been travailing [west] from Nauvoo for nearly a year, and have now arived to the [far] west of the continent of America.

Friday Feb the [12th.] We drilled in the forenoon, and in the afternoon I and Thomas took a walk.

Saturday Feb the 13th. This evening we was inspected.

Sunday Feb. the 14th. There was a me[e]ting today, and this evening.

Monday Feb. the 15th. This company was called out and drilled wi[th] our arms, and equipments an hour in the forenoon and also in the afternoon.

Tuesday Feb. the 16th. We drilled as before and in [the] evening we had a me[e]ting.

Wednesday Feb the 17th. The sun shines beautifull.

Thursday Feb. the 18th. We drilled as before, and in the evening aft[er] tattoo, at half past eight, there was a me[e]ting in our room. Brother Levi Hancock and several others being present, we washed and anointed [one] anothers feet and joints, after which brother Hancock gave some instructions.[15]

---

[15] Forty-three-year-old Levi Ward Hancock was enrolled in Company E as a lowly musician, but as the only Mormon Church general authority to serve with the command his instructions on any subject were the last word for Smith and the faithful volunteers. He was one of seven members of the

Friday Feb. the 19th. We drilled, and in [the] evening some flour and beans, arived at quarters.

Saturday Feb. the 20th. This morning we had flour ten oz. pr day, and Beans dealt out to us for five days, and beaf two pound pr day for three days.

Sunday Feb the 21st. At nine oclock this morning there was an inspection, after which the Ajitant read some of the Law. About eleven oclock there was a me[e]ting and brother Tyler addressed us.[16] This morning some teams started for Sandiego after flour, Sugar and coffee &c., receaving news that a ship load had ariven there.

Tuesday Feb the 23d. Yesterday and today we drilled as before, an hour in the forenoon and also an hour in the afternoon.

Wednesday Feb the 24th. Today we drawed four days rations, of flour twelve oz. (bread and all) and a few beans pr day. And this evening we had a dress parade haveing drilled twice a day for some time. The Battalion makes a pretty good show.

Thursday Feb the 25th. I am on guard today and there is five prisoners in charge.[17]

First Council of the Seventy who represent when traveling the highest authority of the church, at that time Brigham Young. His exercise of this calling eventually put him at odds with some of the Mormon officers who resented his interference in military matters. The zealous New Englander held his office for forty-seven years until his death in 1882.

[16] Daniel Tyler was thirty when he served as a sergeant in Company C and kept the record that enabled him later to produce the book, *A Concise History of the Mormon Battalion in the Mexican War*, published in 1881. If neither concise nor unbiased, the New Yorker's work is useful and continues to influence historians. As he himself reports, he held forth this day on "revering the name of the Deity and avoiding sin of every kind." The battalion chronicler died at Beaver, Utah, in 1906, a few days short of his ninetieth birthday.

[17] Three of this number landed in the guardhouse for killing a cow that belonged to an Indian. A fourth, John Borrowman, Company B, was awaiting a court-martial for sleeping on duty.

Friday Feb. the 26th. This morning at nine oclock I was released from guard; and the wagons that went to Sandiego after provision came to day, and we drawed Sugar and coffee.

Saturday Feb the 27th. Today was spent in police dutys.

Sunday Feb. the 28th. This morning there was a jeneral muster and we were inspected very close by the Colonel.

Monday March the 1st. We drilled as before.

Tuesday March the 2nd. While we were drilling this afternoon the bells in the Catholic Church rung for nearly an hour and sounded most beautifull. After being dismissed from the drill I went in the Church and there was twelve images which looks very nice.

Wednesday March the 3d. This afternoon some more provision arived from Sandiego; one wagon broke and did not get in today.

Thursday March the 4th. We had sugar, coffee, beans, flour &c. dealt out to us for four days, and this evening we had a dress parade.

Saturday March the 6th. We drilled as before and through the day we play ball and amuse ourselves the best way we can. It is very cool weather and clothing scarce.

Sunday March the 7th. We had a dress parade; and the Colonel drilled Company A awhile and then got mad and quit.[18]

Saturday March the 13th. For four days back we have been drilling, as usial. We are now in messes of six. Today we had a Battalion drill, and exercises on fireing wheeling &c.

Sunday March the 14th. This morning there was a jeneral inspection as usial.

---

[18] The next day several noncommissioned officers were reduced to the rank of private for failing to master the drill.

A neglected Spanish mission at San Diego, now restored, is shown in this early photograph much as it appeared in 1847 when Mormon troops camped there. Courtesy of California State Library, California Section.

Monday March the 15th. This morning with two hours notice Company B. left Sanlouis Ray and the other four Companies, not knowing when we would see them again, for Sandiego and travailed 15 miles and encamped.[19]

Wednesday March the 17th. Yesterday we travailed twenty miles, and in the night we dug for water till very late and some of the men

---

[19] Company B's march followed the arrival of Captain Henry S. Turner at San Luis Rey the day before with orders for Cooke to take command of the southern California district under Kearny's authority, at last confirmed by Washington, as chief of land operations on the Pacific Coast and military governor of California. With the command structure finally clear, Cooke moved at once to establish his own authority. He sent Company B to San Diego where it relieved a small dragoon detachment under Lieutenant Stoneman and marched himself for Los Angeles several days later with the other four Mormon companies and Stoneman's dragoons to put Frémont's volunteer battalion under his control and set up headquarters for the newly created district. These developments marked the beginning of Frémont's downfall. See Cooke, *The Conquest of New Mexico and California*, 284–93; *Message from the President on California and New Mexico*, Sen. Ex. Doc. 18, Jan. 24, 1850, S. D. 557, 268–78.

went two mile[s] and a half after water being dry. This morning we travailed about eight miles when we came to Sandiego.[20]

Thursday March the 18th. The marines went on board the Frigate or Man of war Congress.[21]

Saturday March the 20th. I with some others went down to the Ship. She was well finished, ready for war, haveing upward of Sixty can[n]on on board some 26, 32 and 62 pounders, &c. The marines and crew was very sociable, showing us diferent parts of the Ship.[22]

Sunday March the 21st. Eighteen of the company is now quartering at a fort on a high hill east of Sandiego.[23]

---

[20] On its arrival, Company B camped at the foot of Presidio Hill, near the town, some six miles west of the mission on the San Diego River. The settlement then included a few dozen adobe houses and a population of several hundred Spanish and Americans. Much of the early history of San Diego is preserved today at Old Town State Historic Park and Presidio Park.

[21] The marines returned to their ship, the U.S. frigate *Congress*, after manning the defensive works on Presidio Hill, then known as Fort Stockton, which mounted at least seven pieces of artillery. Noting that men from the ship were "Garris[on]ing A fort & some was quartered in the town," Albert Smith said, "A few days after we came all the mariens and salers went A bo[a]rd." See Albert Smith Journal, March 18, 1847.

[22] Then Commodore Stockton's flagship, the *Congress,* was the last of the sailing frigates designed for the U.S. Navy and the top of the line in that class. Mounting forty-four guns, mostly thirty-two-pounders, the warship displaced 1,867 tons and carried a full complement of about 500. Albert Smith said the frigate's guns "in number & Sise looked like enought to Sink the Ship." Launched in 1841 at Portsmouth Navy Yard, the wooden vessel in 1862 was sunk in Hampton Roads by the Confederate ironclad steam ram, *Virginia*, formerly the *Merrimac*.

[23] Before Company B occupied Presidio Hill, the fortifications had changed hands several times. First, Captain Samuel F. Dupont of the twenty-two-gun U.S. warsloop *Cyane* put men ashore in July 1846, to claim the Mexican fort constructed on the ruins of the old presidio, naming it Fort Dupont. Soon after, California insurgents recovered the position and held it until November when Commodore Stockton recaptured it with 100 marines from the *Congress*, then modestly named the fort after himself.

Monday March the 22nd. I and Father went down to the Ocean to bathe and as we were a comeing back the ship Savannah[24] came in sight around a point which extended out into the Pacific west of Sandiego.

Tuesday March the 23d. Brothers Owens, Lawson, Borrowman[25] and myself went about four miles to the coast after mustles, and saw some of the wonderfull works of nature; I also caught twenty three fine fish averageing over a pound apeace.

Monday March the 29th. Last friday the ship Savannah left and just before she started, she fired several rounds which made the air ring. Last evening just before dusk a child of Mr Warners which had died was taken to the grave[26]; two indians carried the corps on their heads and a couple [of] young ladies one on either side with a candle burning. In this way the corps was borne to the grave, and after being placed in the grave the Gentlemen and Ladies help cover it by pawing the dirt in with their hands. Today I and Father went down to the coast and ran races, jumped and sung songs for the first time since we left Nauvoo.

---

[24] The forty-four-gun U.S. frigate *Savannah* and its crew had taken an active part in the military occupation of California from the capture of Monterey in July 1846, to the Battle of Los Angeles six months later when sailors from the ship served under Kearny as foot soldiers. "My Jacks," the general proudly called them. Flagship of the Pacific Squadron, the *Savannah,* displaced 1,726 tons, carried a complement of 480, and took twenty-two years to build at New York Navy Yard.

[25] John Borrowman, thirty, a native of Scotland, was still celebrating his good fortune in avoiding any punishment for sleeping on guard a few weeks before. Cooke had given permission for a battalion court-martial to try the case, but remitted as "excessively lenient" even the token punishment the offender's fellow religionists imposed. The case should have come before a court "whose power extended to the life of the criminal," the colonel said, vowing not to trust the Zionists again. In the meantime, Borrowman took the outcome as a "direct answer to prayer," which was "doubtless correct," remarked Sergeant Tyler. See Tyler, *Concise History,* 268.

[26] Probably a child of John J. Warner of Warner's Ranch and his wife, Anita (daughter of William A. Gale, one of the earliest New England traders to California), who were married in 1837 at San Luis Rey.

Wednesday March the 31st. Yesterday we drilled, and today I and Father went down to the Ocean a fishing, but had poor luck.

Thursday April the 1st. This morning it rains and feels quite refreshing as it is the first Shower we have had for a long time. We have not much to do at present, and I feel very lonesum and want to see home but comfort myself thinking that it is only a little more than three months more till our discharge.

Thursday April the 8th. The week past has been a very lonesum one to me, and yesterday I and Thomas went down to the Coast again, and there are fish in the Ocean which have a stinger on the tail. We went in swiming and one of them stung Thomas on the foot, and he was in great pain four or five hours when it ceased to pain him, and got well. Another Ship came in [the] harbour today.

Thursday April the 15th. The Ship which arived haveing brought more flour we draw a pound to the man. Yesterday I herded the mules and today I am on guard.

Friday April the 16th. Yesterday in the afternoon, there was a man put in irons for shooting at a Spanish man of this place.[27]

Sunday April the 18th. Yesterday I went a fishing and today to a Catholic me[e]ting.

Monday April the 26th. There are more or less Indians in the stocks or under guard all the time. There has another Ship come in harbour lately.

Thursday April the 29th. Day before yesterday Captain Hunters wife died and was buried down to the beach.[28] Father is now make-

---

[27] The offender was not a member of the battalion.

[28] Twenty-three-year-old Lydia Hunter had been married to Captain Jesse Hunter only fifteen months when she died during an influenza epidemic about two weeks after giving birth to a son they named Diego. She was one of only four or five women who completed the march from Council Bluffs to California and a "most estimable lady" in the eyes of the command.

ing doughbys, at six bits pr. hundred. I have been a bakeing light Bread for two or three days back which is good considering the slap jack that we have to bake otherwise.

Tuesday May the 4th. Today we drew forty two dollars with the sutlers bill for six month pay.

Wednesday May the 12th. Yesterday Albert Dunham died and was buried down at the beach,[29] but I made a pair of Shoes. Two men which have been under guard for some time was released today; their names were Johnson and Russel.[30]

Saturday May the 15th. Yesterday there was a Spaniard put under guard for stealing and we have a double guard; and we hung a large Bell up, which is to be rung every night at eight oclock, and a patrole sent out to disperse gatherings and prevent disturbances in the place, and there was catrages dealt out to the company, So to be ready for any thing up, (as the captain expresses it). Today I am on guard and this evening a Spanish child was buried in the most splendid style. The corps was carried on a table, adorned in the most splendid manner which was caried by women, and an Indian with the coffin followed in the croud, two fidlers going in front of the Priest kept fidling. Two men in the rear with rifles kept fireing over their heads.

Sunday May the 16th. The mail arived today with several letters, and they also state that the boys at Purbelow had had a fight with the Indians and killed six.[31] Two of the brethren got wounded. This evening I wrote a letter to Mother.

---

[29] Private Dunham was stricken two or three days before by an ailment diagnosed as "an ulcer on the brain." He was buried near Lydia Hunter's grave.

[30] Not listed on the Company B roster, these men may have belonged to naval units in the area.

[31] With the results Smith describes, Lieutenant Samuel Thompson and twenty men of Company C, stationed at Los Angeles, had executed Cooke's order on March 8 to make "every effort to destroy" some hostile Indians at a nearby ranch in the foothills. Earlier, Kearny reported that Indians in the region had become "very troublesome" because they had been "badly treated by most of the Californians . . . and think they are entitled to what they can steal and rob from them."

Wednesday May the 19th. Yesterday there was a man maried by the name of Barker[32] and in the evening they had a dance, and performed very well.

Sunday May the 23d. This morning there was an inspection, after which we brought up two cannon and some balls from the quarters that the marines left. The weather is beautifull and every thing goes on very well, but still this is not a home to me.

> and I think thus.

1. Oh my home when shall I see thee,
   And the friends I love so well,
   I do not like this barren country
   But glad would bid it long farewell.
   > Let me hasten,
   To the home I love so well.

2. My heart feels sad I cant forget thee,
   While I love thy scenes so well,
   Haste kind heaven and restore me,
   To the home I love so well.
   > Let me hasten
   To the home I love so well.
   > Or in other words.

1. On the Pacific Ocean some thousand miles from home,
   Across the rocky mountains I had a cause to roam,
   Enlisting for a soldier and leave my native land,
   And with my friends and kindred I took the parting hand.

2. Far from my dear Mother and Sisters I am,
   But by the grace of God I will see them again,
   And live in Zions city most glorious to behold,
   Whose walls are made of jasper and streets of purest
   Gold.

---

[32] Identified by Tyler only as an American sea captain who took a California bride in a Catholic Church ceremony, the groom may have been John S. Barker, master of the New Bedford whaler *Edward* whose crew took part in the American occupation and later fought Mexican forces in Lower California. There was also a Peruvian bark on the California coast at this time with a captain named Barker. See Tyler, *Concise History*, 285.

3. With thanks and adoration to God forever more,
   And sing a song of Zion, the great I am adore,
   When the lamb and the Lion together shall lie down,
   Then Christ will be the standard and nations flock
       around.

Friday May the 28th. The week past has passed of[f] so far very well; however Sunday evening about thirty Indians came here in arms but it was for a good motive, hearing that the Captain had Sent for them. The boys are byeing mules and horses nearly every day, and I sent out for one this morning; they are jenerally from five to fifteen dollars.[33]

Sunday May the 30th. Today I weighed one hundred and thirty two pounds, the most I ever weighed in my life.

Friday June the 4th. Yesterday I went down to the coast, with the team which went after ten barrels of flour. There are ships in harbour being merchant Ships.

Wednesday June the [9th.] A few days ago I and father bought us each a horse, those haveing arived which we sent for. Yesterday I had my coat stolen.

Monday June the 14th. Last week I went after some oats which gr[ow] Spontaneous on the hills, and Fathers Mare got away from me with Thomases Sad[d]le on her back; and is not found yet. Yesterday I and Thomas went again after oats and packed it in on our horses.

Saturday June 19th. This week [on] Tuesday Father got a furlough and took my mare and sad[d]le, and went to look for his, and has not got [back] but I think he will be back today. The four com-

---

[33] Having been paid on May 4, Company B members were engaged in buying livestock and clothing to prepare for the journey to rejoin their families. Many, such as Albert Smith, took outside work making bricks, building houses, or digging wells to earn extra money.

panys which are at [Purbelow] are building a fort,[34] with the help of the dragoons which they have [almost] completed. Colonel Cooke with others haveing started for the [States] Mr. Stevenson is promoted to colonel and we expect him here to[day].[35]

Thursday June the 24th. The Colonel has arived and is high[ly] [satisfied with] us, and is desirous that we should re-enlist; and the Captain with some twenty men have volunteers for Six months.[36] Some are for him, and some for the council of the Preisthood which we have

---

[34] While Company B members hired themselves out to earn extra money at San Diego, the other four companies at Los Angeles Pueblo ("Purbelow" as Smith called it) were put to work on the less rewarding task of building a fort on the hill that overlooked the town and anchorage. The position was dedicated on July 4, 1847, and named in honor of First Dragoons Captain Benjamin D. Moore of Kentucky, who was lanced to death at the Battle of San Pasqual. What was left of Fort Moore Hill, following construction of the Hollywood Freeway, is now occupied by the Los Angeles City Board of Education. The Fort Moore Pioneer Wall was dedicated on the site in 1958. See *Fort Moore Pioneer Memorial, Dedication Ceremonies, July 3, 1958*, Utah State Historical Society.

[35] The battalion's new commander, Colonel Jonathan D. Stevenson, was a forty-seven-year-old New York politician who had little in common with the career soldier he replaced on April 28. But he soon won commendation for the discipline of his regiment, the First New York Volunteers, which had arrived by sea in March, and his handling of occupation duties that were often more political in nature than military. Cooke, at his own request, was relieved of duty and returned overland with General Kearny and a twelve-man Mormon Battalion escort to Fort Leavenworth for reassignment in a party that included John C. Frémont and the unpopular "Dr. Death," George Sanderson. On the day he arrived, August 22, the general would place Frémont under arrest for his mutinous conduct in California, a prelude to the explorer's famous court-martial and resignation. Sanderson also left the army on his arrival at the Missouri River base.

[36] Facing a serious shortage of troops, Stevenson did his utmost to reenlist the Mormons who were known for good conduct and high tolerance to the temptation to desert. His promise to allow officers to choose the new battalion commander at the rank of lieutenant colonel if their companies signed up caused a split in Mormon ranks. The number from Company B who initially offered to extend their service reflected the popularity of Captain Jesse D. Hunter, who had commanded from the beginning.

with us.[37] I am one of the latter. Day before yesterday I went down to the Ship and bought some clothing of the hands; they were very kind and gave us some dinner.

Thursday July the 1st. The Captain has gone to Purbelow to make out his company there.[38] We are at present busy prepareing to start back home.

Monday July the 5th. Night before last after midnight, some of the Boys, with their muskets went round to the officers and Don Magill, Mr Vansenys and other friendly Spaniards,[39] saluting them by fireing and giveing them cheers; they all treated them, and felt well pleased. The boys got prety high, and some of them came in our room after catrages, and some of them stole two dollars worth of Sugar, which I and Father bought, but we got some of it back, finding it hid outdoors. We believe Zabrisky[40] to be the one that took it. Last evening the Captain returned. I beleave he ran again[st] a

---

[37] Stevenson later reported that the Mormons were "entirely under the control of their leaders" and there were "two men," referring to Hancock and Pettegrew, "who were the chief men; and but for them, at least three companies would have re-enlisted." See Stevenson to Mason, July 23, 1847, in Sen. Doc. 18, 31st Cong., 1st sess., 1849–50, vol. 9, 337–38.

[38] Sergeant William Hyde and Corporal Horace Alexander also went to Los Angeles where they opposed Hunter in a heated exchange over the issue of reenlistment. Given a choice between officers on one side and church authority and families on the other, most chose church and family, but enough elected to sign up for six more months, including thirteen from Company B, to form a new Mormon company that would be stationed at San Diego.

[39] Of the two named, the first was probably Don Miguel Pedrorena, about thirty-eight, an educated Spaniard who had come to San Diego by way of Peru and married into an influential family; the other may have been Juan Bandini, a noted political leader. Both had sided early with the Americans.

[40] Nineteen-year-old Private Jerome Zabriskie from Indiana was one of about eighty-five who reenlisted. He later settled at Provo, Utah, where he and two other battalion veterans, Richard Ivie and Rufus Stoddard, touched off the territory's first Indian war in 1849 when they killed a native for stealing a shirt. He eventually located at Minersville where he died in 1904.

snag at Purbelow and is not like[ly] to make out his Company.[41] The boys gave the Captain and other officers, cheers again last night. In two or three days we are to go to Purbelow for our discharge.

Wednesday July the 14th. We are now within about fifteen miles of Purbelow, haveing left Sandiego on the 9th. and have travailed about twenty miles a day. I have been unwell for a day or two but feel better today.[42]

Tuesday, July 20th. We arived at Purbelow on the fifteenth, and stayed there three days, and got our discharge. On the 19th. I and Father took our provision, and animals about three miles above Purbelow on a creek where, brother Levi Hancock and those that are going back home are gathering.[43] There is a company made up of Mormon volunteers, at Purbelow, (and Thomas has enlisted).[44] They was today mustered into service. Davis is captain and Canfield, Barnas, and Clift are Lieutenants.[45] There has a company started

---

[41] Having failed to sign up a command of his own or to win election to head the only company to reenlist, Hunter at the end of his term of service accepted an appointment by Governor Mason as Indian agent at San Luis Rey Mission. He remained in California and died in 1882 at Los Angeles.

[42] Not one to complain, Smith fails to mention the reason for his illness, but his father later told what happened during the march to Los Angeles and the unfortunate aftermath: "the Second day after we started Azariah was throad from [h]is mare by her jumping Stiff leg[g]ed he fell on [h]is head on the hard pavement he suf[f]ered from the hurt all but de[a]th [For] too years he had most of the time A tarible headake then it terminated in fits. The fits contin[u]ed with him fifteen years." See Albert Smith Journal, 38.

[43] The ranking church official, Hancock directed the largest body of battalion veterans who gathered on the Los Angeles River and formed into companies. He appointed and the party unanimously endorsed former Company E lieutenants James Pace and Andrew Lytle as captains of hundreds; William Hyde, Daniel Tyler, and Reddick Allred, former sergeants, as captains of fifties; and Elisha Averett and T. C. D. Howells, among others, as captains of tens. The names of other unit leaders were unrecorded.

[44] Thomas Dutcher, brother of Azariah Smith's mother, Esther.

[45] The former captain of Company E, forty-three-year-old Daniel C. Davis, was elected to command the new company made up of those who reenlisted. A native New Yorker, Davis later settled in Utah where a county

for the Bay of Francisco also today called Dikes'es Company.[46] We bought one hundred and Seventy pounds of flour, (brand and all) yesterday and Father sifted it last night; it cost us $3.50 pr hundred but there is considerable waste in sifting. We have three mares one mule and one horse, between us, which I think will do us.

We drawed thirty one dollars and a half to the man Yesterday morning and are now our own men.

---

north of Salt Lake City was named after him. The other officers at the rank of lieutenant were Cyrus Canfield, thirty, Ruel Barrus, thirty-four, and Robert Clift, twenty-three, former lieutenants of companies D, B and C, respectively.

[46] A smaller party followed former Company A Captain Jefferson Hunt north on the Spanish mission trail to San Francisco Bay, thence to Sutter's Fort where it arrived at about the same time as Hancock's discharged veterans. As Smith suggests, the disliked George Dykes, former adjutant and Company D lieutenant, may have been among the Hunt group.

4

GOLD AT SUTTER'S MILL
July 28, 1847–June 22, 1848

As advance elements of Brigham Young's pioneer company entered the valley of Great Salt Lake, the largest body of Mormon veterans of the War with Mexico, more than 150 strong, broke camp on the Los Angeles River and started north on the trail to Mission San Fernando Rey de España. Azariah Smith on July 21, 1847, was at last going home—or so he thought.

Several days before, the members of the most remarkable military unit ever to serve the American republic had been mustered out with little ceremony at Los Angeles. They had been given their arms and accoutrements, as promised by General Kearny, plus twenty-one rounds of ammunition each and recognition as exceptional as the force itself.

For the "patience, subordination, and general good conduct" of the battalion during the occupation of California, Colonel Richard B. Mason, the military governor, was outspoken in his praise. From local inhabitants, "not a syllable of complaint has reached my ears of a single insult offered, or outrage done, by a Mormon volunteer," Mason reported.[1] Compared with the behavior of other American volunteers during the war, it was a singular record.

After a year of service, Smith and his companions no longer belonged to the U.S. Army, but as members of a closely organized religious culture, they were hardly their "own men," as the teenager exulted. So it was that the veterans of companies A through E, American Army of the West, now marched in companies of ten, fifty, and

---

[1] R. B. Mason to R. Jones, September 18, 1847, in Sen. Doc. 18, 31st Cong., 1st sess., 1849–50, vol. 9, 318–22.

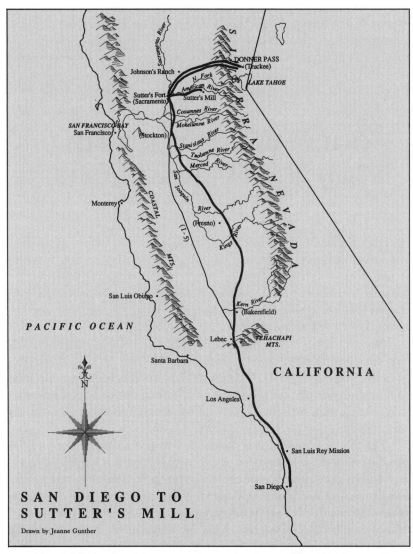

SAN DIEGO TO
SUTTER'S MILL

Drawn by Jeanne Gunther

one hundred, each with a captain at the head, like the hosts of ancient Israel, the prescribed traveling order of the Kingdom of God.

Unlike other volunteers who completed their enlistments that year
and went home, none of the Mormon veterans started out with a sure
idea of where his home was to be found. More than ten months had
passed since any word had come from the leaders of their faith on
the whereabouts of their families or what the final destination of the
move west might be.

Many of those who volunteered to serve for six more months as garrison troops at San Diego did so in the expectation that their fellow religionists would eventually come to the West Coast. Among terms they proposed as conditions of reenlistment was that at the end of their service they would receive travel pay and rations to the place of their choice, either "the Salt lake, into which Bear river empties," or the Bay of San Francisco.[2]

Behind this condition was the awareness that Elder Samuel Brannan and some 230 members of the faith had sailed into San Francisco Bay a full year before on the ship *Brooklyn* to settle in California. Already, the Mormon arrivals had planted a communal farming colony to the north, called New Hope.

According to former sergeant William Hyde, battalion veterans also knew that the twenty-eight-year-old promoter even then was on his way to meet Brigham Young on the high plains. Brannan, who would become California's first millionaire, hoped to guide Young and his pioneer company back over the Sierra Nevada to the agricultural paradise that he had discovered near the delta of the San Joaquin and Sacramento rivers.[3]

Whatever these developments portended, the men who had left the army were unwilling to wait for events to take their course. Anxious to rejoin their loved ones, they set out to find them wherever they had to go from the Pacific Ocean to the Missouri River.

Those who comprised the main company under church general authority Levi Hancock, including Smith and his father, journeyed north on the line of today's Interstate 5 toward Tejón Pass in the Tehachapi Mountains, first crossed in 1772 by the acting Spanish governor of Alta California, Pedro Fages. A somewhat smaller party with the battalion's senior captain, Jefferson Hunt, took the longer but more heavily traveled Spanish mission road, *El Camino Real*, along the coast.

By different routes, they headed for the western terminal of a new wagon road, a fledgling center of commerce and trade at the confluence of the American and Sacramento rivers, founded eight years before by a thirty-six-year-old Swiss visionary who could never live within his means. Already deeply in debt, he was about to jump into

---

[2] J. D. Stevenson to R. B. Mason, July 27, 1847, Ibid., 336–37.

[3] See Paul Bailey, *Sam Brannan and the California Mormons* (Los Angeles: Westernlore Press, 1943).

John Augustus Sutter, founder of New Helvetia at age thirty-six and ruler of the little empire of commerce and industry centered at Sutter's Fort at the confluence of the Sacramento and American rivers. Courtesy of California State Library, California Section.

a new venture with a moody partner from New Jersey, named James Marshall, to build a sawmill on the South Fork of the American River.

John Augustus Sutter named his wilderness kingdom, on vast grants of Mexican land, New Helvetia, or New Switzerland. But the traders and immigrants who always found hospitality and employment there called it Sutter's Fort after the central trading post, built where Sacramento now stands, with adobe brick walls eighteen feet high, a compound 320 feet long and two bastions, five feet thick, mounted with cannons.[4]

---

[4] For the story of Sutter, see Richard Hugh Dillon, *Fool's Gold, the Decline and Fall of Captain John Sutter of California* (New York: Coward-McCann, 1967), reissued in paperback as *Captain John Sutter: Sacramento Valley's Sainted Sinner* (Santa Cruz, Calif.: Western Tanager Press, 1981, 1987).

To Sutter's Fort the Mormon companies would go unless they could find a better way over the mountains than the primitive road by Donner Pass and along the Truckee River, first traveled by wagons only three years before. There they would rest and refit before pushing on with their faces to the morning sun until they found their people, somewhere to the east. And so it would come about—for most of them.

But for Azariah Smith and a few, the domain of Captain Sutter, as he liked to be called, was to be more than a resting place. For there they would become participants in an event so significant it would touch the life of nearly everyone in the United States and trigger a massive population shift west. It was the discovery of gold![5]

[The Journal]

Wednesday July the 28th. We travailed forty miles in two days crossing a very bad mountain and encamped on a small creek and good springs;[6] we stayed there four days and waited for the rear to come up; we also bought forty head of beef cattle, at six dollars a head, and today we started with much trouble, every one haveing as much as he well could take care of and then had to furnish a man out of each ten for cattle guard, they being very wild and twelve of them got away today haveing a very bad mountain to cross, worse than I can describe, being very steep, long and tegeous [tedious]. After geting to the top of the mountain we came in[to] a small vally and litt[l]e water, and poor as well as little feed for our horses.

---

[5] Sources on this historic event include Rodman W. Paul, *The California Gold Discovery, Sources, Documents, Accounts and Memoirs Relating to the Discovery of Gold at Sutter's Mill* (Georgetown, Calif.: Talisman Press, 1966); J. Kenneth Davies, *Mormon Gold, The Story of California's Mormon Argonauts* (Salt Lake City: Olympus Publishing Co., 1984); Norma Baldwin Ricketts, *Mormons and the Discovery of Gold*, 3d ed. (Sacramento: Ricketts Publishing Co., 1982); and Wade Lillywhite, *The Mormons and the Discovery of Gold in California, A List of Sixteen Important Publications* (Salt Lake City: Utah Westerners, 1985).

[6] The company followed the Spanish trail to San Fernando Mission, near the present city of the same name, then continued to Rancho San Francisco on the Santa Clara River, near today's junction of Interstate 5 and State Highway 126. Here they rested and purchased cattle from Antonio del Valle who had acquired the 48,600-acre ranch in 1839.

Friday July the 30th. On the night of the twenty eighth I was on cattle guard, and we had to be on horseback, as the cattle were very uneasy, not haveing any water, and would charge on footmen.

Yesterday we came through and over mountains, and in some places the pass would be so narrow that our pack horses could hardly get through, and on either side some hundreds of feet nearly perpendicular. We travailed about fifteen miles and encamped about thirty miles from where we camped on the creek. Today we remained at this place and killed all the beaf cattle, (about twenty six in number,) and cut them up to dry. Ther is two beafs in our mess of eleven.

Tuesday August the 3d. Saturday we dried our beaf and Sunday we travailed sixteen miles and encamped in the mountains by a pret[t]y creek.[7] Monday we travailed twenty five miles being part of the way on a large vally.[8] Four Indians came to camp this morning and two of them travailed with us today, we travailed about fourteen miles and encamped on a river.[9]

Friday August the 6th. On the fourth we crossed the river. I with some others crossed at a ford with our horses, others crossed above and swam their horses, and built a float to take their things across on. Yesterday we travailed thirty miles and encamped in the mountains, with very lit[t]le water for our horses. Today we travailed ten miles and encamped in the mountains with plenty of water and feed.

---

[7] A pioneer party left a day earlier and on August 1 camped at the present town of Lebec in Grapevine Canyon where Henry Bigler reported finding the inscription on a tree: "Peter Lebeck who was killed by a Bear Oct. 17, 1837." Smith fails to mention his nineteenth birthday on August 1.

[8] After crossing the Tehachapi Mountains, the company entered the southern end of California's Great Central Valley, nearly 500 miles long and some 50 miles wide, bordered on the east by the Sierra Nevada and to the west by the Coastal range. The valley is drained from the south by the San Joaquin River, which flows north, and from the north by the Sacramento River, which flows south. Both rivers empty into San Francisco Bay.

[9] This was the Kern River, named by Frémont in 1845 after his artist and topographer, Edward M. Kern, which was crossed near present Bakersfield. Its earliest European name was Rio de San Felipe, given in 1776 by the Franciscan missionary, Francisco Tomás Hermenegido Garcés.

Saturday August the 7th. We travailed eighte[en] miles when we came to a strip of timber and water in holes.[10]

Sunday Aug the 8th. We travailed eight miles when we came to a creek and a few Indians which gave us some information. We camped here about eleven oclock. The camp is in good spirits and ma[ny] of the animals doing well. We are now two hundred three miles from Purbelow.

Monday Aug the 9th. Last night I was on guard as there are a great many Indians and hostile. We travailed twenty fiv[e] miles and encamped on a river with good feed.[11]

Tuesday Aug the 10th. This morning while the most of the company was floating their things across, a few of us packed ours across on a log [and] swam our horses. After travailing ten miles we encamped.

Wednesday Aug the 11th. We travailed twenty eight miles across a plain and I got very dry.[12]

Thursday Aug the 12th. We layed by, and some of the pioneers went to find a pass over to the Basin.[13] There are a good many In-

---

[10] The company probably took the old Tulare Trail, now generally followed by State Highway 65 from Bakersfield to Exeter, which would place this camp near present Porterville on the Tule River.

[11] This river was the Kaweah, named for a tribe of Yokut Indians, where they probably camped at the ford about seven miles east of present Visalia.

[12] Many were stricken by thirst before they reached Kings River at a point several miles east of present Fresno. As each party arrived at the stream, reported Henry Bigler, "their canteens were taken and filled and sent back to their comrades, and thus the sufferers were relieved." See *Bigler's Chronicle*, 66.

[13] Apparently misled by the map they were following, leaders sent an exploring party up Kings River to look for the pass over the Sierra Nevada to the Great Basin, named for Joseph Reddeford Walker, trapper and guide who made the first recorded crossing in 1832, while the main company camped near the mouth of Kings Canyon. Actually located much to the south, Walker's Pass is crossed today by State Highway 178 between Bakersfield and Freeman Junction.

dians here and a long string of them came to camp, and they was badly frightened and shook like a leaf. They danced some in the forenoon but in the afternoon they took their effects and left.

Friday Aug the 13th. We travailed twelve miles up the river and encamped in the mountains. The pioneers could find no pass and came back.

Saturday Aug the 14th. This morning we backed out and crossed the river and haveing travailed eight miles we encamped. We expect to go across to the Sacramento where there is a wagon road.[14]

Monday Aug the 16th. Yesterday we travailed twelve miles when we stop[p]ed while some of the pioneers went ahead on a mountain to see if they could see water ahead, and seeing a river they fired a gun,[15] but we not hearing it so far off, encamped. When they returned we again packed up and travailed twelve miles farther makeing twenty four miles and encamped on the river. Today we cross the river which was very swift,[16] and travailed seventeen miles and encamped on a small ravine, with no water only by diging holes in the sand.

Friday Aug the 20th. Tuesday we travailed twenty five miles and Wednesday 25 miles when we came to a river,[17] and some Indians which gave us watermellons and green corn which is a rarity in this country. Thursday we travailed twenty five miles, and today we

---

[14] Failing to find a pass, they headed north on the trail mapped by Frémont in 1844 toward Sutter's Fort to cross the mountains at Donner Pass where the Stevens-Townsend-Murphy party had made the first crossing with wagons three years before.

[15] The river they saw was the San Joaquin, which flows west as it emerges from the mountains, named about 1806 by Lieutenant Gabriel Moraga, Spanish soldier and explorer. Moraga's father came to California with Anza and founded the San Francisco presidio in 1776.

[16] Following the Frémont trail, they probably crossed the river at Gravelly Ford, near Herndon. For Frémont's map, which they apparently used, and description of the San Joaquin Valley, see his report, Sen. Doc. 174, 28th Cong., 2nd sess., 1845.

[17] This was probably the Merced River, a tributary of the San Joaquin, also named by Lieutenant Gabriel Moraga after "Our Lady of Mercy."

Sutter's Fort on the site of present Sacramento as seen in 1847 by Azariah Smith and other Mormon Battalion veterans who first came there for supplies, then returned to seek work from Captain Sutter. Courtesy of California State Library, California Section.

travailed twenty five miles and encamped on another river.[18] The rivers in this part of the country is very pret[t]y.

Sunday Aug. the 22nd. Yesterday we travailed fourteen miles, and today we travailed twenty eight miles, and had a bad road for our horses, as some of them are tender footed.

Last night at a me[e]ting four men was apointed to go ahead to Sutters fort and find out the price of horses mules and provision and return tomorrow and meet us.[19] It was also motioned and caried, that

---

[18] They camped on the Stanislaus River, not far from present Ripon, where Indians told them about a settlement of Americans, eight or nine miles downstream. Investigating, Captain Lytle and two others found the little colony of New Hope, established late in 1846 by Samuel Brannan and members of the *Brooklyn* company. The river was named after a runaway mission Indian who led a native uprising against the Spanish in 1829.

[19] On August 23, the members of this party arrived at Sutter's Fort where they learned from one Charles C. Smith that Great Salt Lake Valley, not California, would be the final destination of the Mormon movement west. Smith nearly four months before had gone east over the trail with Samuel Brannan to find Brigham Young and guide his pioneer company to the West Coast. After meeting the Mormon leader at the Oregon

those that their horses had gave out and those that were destitute of provision should be fit[t]ed out in preference to those better off.

Monday Aug. the 23. We travailed fourteen miles.

Tuesday Aug. the 24th. We travailed twenty five miles when we came to a river.[20] Brother Little came in camp with Hunt haveing receaved news from the Church that the Twelve are at Salt Lake with the pioneers; and five hundred wagons are expected there by this time.[21]

Trail crossing of Green River, Smith had headed back alone, meeting members of General Kearny's Mormon Battalion escort on the trail east of Soda Springs and reaching Sutter's Fort on August 23, more than two weeks ahead of the disappointed Brannan who arrived on September 10. See John A. Sutter, *New Helvetia Diary, A Record of Events Kept by John A. Sutter and His Clerks* (San Francisco: Grabhorn Press, 1939), referred to hereafter as *New Helvetia Diary*, 71, 72, 77. Also see Journal of Nathaniel V. Jones, printed in Kate B. Carter, "March of the Mormon Battalion," *Heart Throbs of the West* (Salt Lake City: Daughters of Utah Pioneers, 1946), 7:160, and Tyler, *Concise History*, 310.

[20] The Cosumnes River, a tributary of the Mokelumne, was reached just west of today's crossing of State Highway 99, near Elk Grove, where the company camped on the north bank at Murphy's Ranch, owned by Martin Murphy, Jr., who had come to California in 1844 with the Stevens-Townsend-Murphy party.

[21] Lytle and others, apparently including Jefferson Hunt, told the company what they had learned from Charles Smith about Mormon plans. Little is known about Brannan's self-reliant partner, Smith, except that he had lived as a Mormon in Nauvoo, traveled overland in 1846 to California, and was recognized on June 30, 1847, by one of Brigham Young's pioneer company at Green River as "Smith of the firm of Jackson Heaton & Bonney, bogus makers of Nauvoo," which may explain his early departure from the Mormon camp. The Bonney referred to was Edward Bonney, a bounty hunter at Nauvoo, who claimed the Mormon metropolis was a sanctuary for thieves and counterfeiters and was himself acquitted of making bogus money in December 1846. See William Clayton, *William Clayton's Journal* (Salt Lake City: Clayton Family Association, 1921), June 30, 1847, 281. Also see Edward Bonney, *The Banditti of the Prairies* (Chicago: Steam Press, 1850), reprinted for Western Frontier Library, University of Oklahoma Press, 1963, and Joseph H. Jackson, another of the bogus makers referred

Saturday Aug. the 28th. Last Wednesday we layed by, and Thursday we travailed about twenty three miles to another river[22] and encamped five miles from Sutters fort. Friday we again layed by for the purpose of geting our horses shod, and we are also laying by today for the same purpose.[23]

Wednesday Sept. the 1st. Last Sunday we travailed eighteen miles and monday twenty two miles, and got two of our horses shod, and bought some wheat and peas.[24] Yesterday we travailed twenty two miles turning an easterly direction in to the mountains. Today we travailed fourteen miles farther. Some of the horses are geting thin.

Thursday Sept. the 2nd. We travailed eighteen miles being in the largest mountains we have to cross, which are very steep. There are small vallys on the top of the mountains and very cold Springs. We encamped by one of them.

Saturday Sept the 4th. Yesterday we travailed thirteen miles and encamped on Bear Creek, in a vally called Little Bear Vally.[25]

---

to, *A Narrative of the Adventures and Experience of Joseph H. Jackson in Nauvoo* (Warsaw, Ill., 1844), reprinted by Karl Yost, Morrison, Ill., 1960, copy at Utah State Historical Society.

[22] The American River was named by Sutter after a ford called "El Paso de Los Americanos" by Spanish-speaking Indians where early trappers crossed. Bigler said he camped on the north bank, but the fort was located on the south, or opposite shore.

[23] Horses were shod at Sutter's Fort for $1 per shoe. While some battalion veterans elected to stay and work for $25 to $60 a month, considered good wages, most headed north as their companies were already toward the last settlement before the Sierra Nevada, owned by William Johnson, an American sailor, who had acquired the property in 1845.

[24] Supplies and a blacksmith were found at Johnson's Ranch on Bear River, some three miles east of present Wheatland, where Donner Party survivors had staggered in less than eight months before with first news of the disaster. The exact location of this historic place was found in 1986 by Jack Steed of Sacramento. See Jack Steed, *The Donner Party Rescue Site, Johnson's Ranch on Bear River* (Fresno, Calif.: Pioneer Publishing Co., 1988).

[25] This camp was located about four miles west of present Emigrant Gap on Interstate 80. See Charles K. Graydon, *Trail of the First Wagons over the Sierra Nevada* (Gerald, Mo.: Patrice Press, 1986).

Today we layed by for our animals to recruit, there being plenty [of] good feed. For a few days we have been travailing through plenty of Pine, Cedar, Hemlock, Redwood, Oak and other timber and some of them very large.

Monday Sept the 6th. Yester[day] we travailed twelve miles. Today we travailed fifteen miles, and just at night, Brothers Brannon and Raney came to camp to hur[ry] us on to the rest of our company about thirty miles ahead, and also Captain Browns company just from Salt Lake vally where [the] church is going to settle.[26]

Tuesday Sept the 7th. We crossed the divide which was very high and snow in places on top. It was sundown before we got to camp. In the evening there was a letter read from the Twelve to the Battalion which gave us much joy.[27] I and Father receaved a letter from mother which gave us much more.

Wednesday Sept the 8th. Acording to council from the Twelve this morning, I with a good many others of our Company turned our course back to California to w[ork] and fit ourselves out ready for the Spring. Father took four of the animals, and most of the provi-

---

[26] Samuel Brannan and twenty-nine-year-old Company B veteran David P. Rainey met Azariah's party at Summit Valley, near present Soda Springs. Brannan was headed to Sutter's Fort from Salt Lake Valley where his final plea had failed to convince Brigham Young to lead his followers to California. Rainey came back from the advance party to urge trailing groups forward for a meeting with Captain James Brown, a battalion officer detached at Santa Fe, who bore instructions from Mormon leaders and letters from families. Brown was on his way to Monterey to claim the mustering out pay of Pueblo battalion members. See *Bigler's Chronicle*, 75–76.

[27] Where Truckee City is now located, the returning veterans gathered to hear news and instructions from their leaders as summarized by Albert Smith: Brigham Young "Counsiled all that had no famlyes to Stay & work one year in California as thare was but A small company coming thrue to Salt lake that fall & it would be an imposibility for them to have any provision for to Spare." Nearby, where Donner party members had perished, "thare bones ware laying scatered over the grownd." See Albert Smith Journal, 40.

sion and went on to put in a crop.[28] After travailing fifte[en] miles we came where there was a sick man [and] encamped with him.

Friday Sept the 10th. Yesterday we travailed thirty miles. Today we travailed twenty five miles. I miss Father and feel very lonesum here in the mountains.

Saturday Sept the 11th. Last night brother Allens[29] two mares strayed away not being staked out. We started early this morning and travailed thirty miles, and saw two indians on the way.

Sunday Sept the 12th. We travailed twenty four miles when we came to Johnsons and encamped.

Monday Sept the 13th. We travailed twenty miles towards Sutters Fort.

Tuesday Sept the 14th. We travailed twenty miles and encamped on the old camping ground five miles from Sutters.

Sunday Sept the 19th. Last Wednesday we took a job of Sutter of dig[g]ing a raceway at 12 1/2 cts pr. square yard,[30] and went about

---

[28] As Albert Smith went on to Salt Lake Valley to find his wife and other children, Azariah and about half of the company obediently turned back to recross Donner Pass and seek work in California, many of them at Sutter's Fort. Not for another year would he be restored to his family.

[29] Why thirty-three-year-old Ezra H. Allen returned to California with this group is unclear since he had left a wife and two children when he enlisted in the battalion as a musician in Company C. The New Yorker was killed, apparently by Indians, on June 27, 1848. For the circumstances of his death, see Smith's journal entry on July 20, 1848, in chapter 5.

[30] Sutter employed all of the veterans who wanted to work for him, offering to pay them $25 per month or 12.5 cents a yard to dig a canal, or millrace, for the gristmill he was building on the left bank of the American River, about three miles east of the fort, on the site now occupied by California State University at Sacramento. The Mormons chose to work by the yard, but the incentive proved too much for some who became "sick on account of their working to[o] hard." See *New Helvetia Diary*, 82.

five miles to a house, to quarter for that purpose. I worked three days and it is hard work, but I guess we will make better than a dollar a day. Sutter furnishes provision, such as Flour, Peas, Beaf &c. and tools to work with.

Friday Sept the 24th. Three days this week I have worked, but my back was so lame yesterday that I did not work.

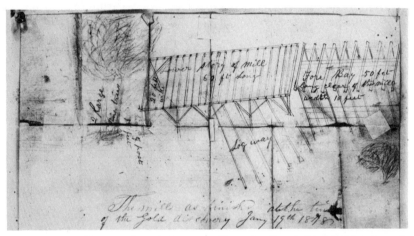

James Marshall's drawing of the sawmill on the South Fork of the American River at present Coloma, California. Courtesy of California State Library, California Section.

Sunday Oct the 3d. Last monday Sutter sent after some hands to go up in the mountains, about thirty miles, to work at his sawmill and I with several others went.[31] We was three days, a going there, as we had an ox team, which was very slow. I got here on Thursday. We have a woman cook which is something we have not had for a

---

[31] Besides Smith, Henry Bigler, twenty-three-year-old William Johnston, and Israel Evans, nineteen, went to work at this time for James Marshall, Sutter's partner in the venture to build a sawmill on the South Fork of American River, about forty trail miles east of Sutter's Fort, and raft lumber downstream. A replica of Sutter's Mill can be seen today at Marshall Gold Discovery Historic State Park in Coloma on State Highway 49 between Auburn and Placerville.

long time.[32] I have had a fever every other day and have not worked any yet. Yesterday and today I have been takeing pills.

Monday Oct the 4th. The ague passed by, agreable to my wishes and may God grant me health untill I return to my Father, Mother, Sisters, and Brother. I feel like a cat in a strange garrit, but hope I will be able to go at work in a few days and wont feel quite so lonesum.

Monday Oct the 11th. By Thursday I thought I had got well, and anxious to procure means to take me back home, in the morning I went to work, and worked lightly till noon when after dinner I had a chill, and have had one every day since, but I think I am a geting better, and trust the Lord will raise me to health.

Sunday Oct the 17th. Through the goodness of the Lord my chil[l]s have left me but I have been very weak. One night before the chills left I was very sick, and I felt bad the thought running in my mind that likely I never should see home again which was a perfect torment to my mind, but when I got over my chills I reconciled my mind a little better. I find the Lord a true friend in time of need. My strength is now so I can just nicely walk. Mrs. Wimmer the woman that cooks uses me kindly for which I hope she will receave a reward.

---

[32] The cook and housekeeper for the workmen was the spirited Elizabeth Jane "Jennie" Wimmer who had come overland to California in 1846 with her thirty-six-year-old husband, Peter, and seven children by former marriages of both. As members of the Harlan-Young Party, they were among the first to take wagons over the Hastings Cutoff, making the Salt Desert crossing south of Great Salt Lake just ahead of the disaster-bound Donner–Reed Party. Peter Wimmer supervised Indian laborers at the project. The family lived in one end of a double log cabin while the hired hands, including Smith and five other Mormons, slept in the other. See W. W. Allen and R. B. Avery, *California Gold Book, First Nugget, Its Discovery and Discoverers* (San Francisco: Donohue & Henneberry, 1893), 11–68; and Bruce R. Hawkins and David B. Madsen, *Excavation of the Donner-Reed Wagons: Historic Archaeology along the Hastings Cutoff* (Salt Lake City: University of Utah Press, 1990), 22–29.

Friday Oct the 22nd. I am very weak, but gain a little with the help of the Lord, and the kindness of Mrs. Wimmer.[33]

Monday November the 1st. Through the past week a part of the time we were out of flour, and had nothing but wheat, peas, and mutton, without salt. But Friday a wagon came with [a] lit[t]le Flour, salt, Pumpkins, &c. and last night Mr. Marshall came with some more provision. I am gaining my health pret[t]y fast.

Wednesday Nov. the 10th. I am still gaining, and through the week past I hunted some after deer, and saw two but did not get a shot. I went more for exercise than any thing else. Last Sunday brother Bigler killed a small fawn,[34] which went fine. We have a good deal of rain.

Sunday Nov. the 14th. The past week I made pins for the mill.

Sunday Nov. the 21st. The week past I have been to work by the day boreing, and martaceing timber. Yesterday there came five wagon loads of provision, as the provision for the winter, has to be bro[ught] before the rainy season commences.[35]

Sunday Nov the 28th. The week has passed off pret[t]y busy, and the mill goes ahead a good job; we have part of the dam in, and the bents, and plates of the lower story raised.

Sunday Dec. the 5th. The past week I have been driving [team]. Yesterday two wagon loads of provision came from Sutters.

---

[33] Smith's feelings toward Jennie Wimmer would change as the sharp-tongued cook adopted other favorites and insisted that her wards show up for meals on time.

[34] Marshall entrusted his rifle "(and he had a good one)" to Henry Bigler who hunted game for the camp when the meat supply became short. See *Bigler's Chronicle*, 84.

[35] Besides pumpkin, apparently Smith's favorite, food supplies at the project consisted mainly of unbolted flour, pork, mutton, salmon, peas, tea, coffee, and sugar.

Sunday Dec. the 12th. Last Thursday I had a chill and fever. I have not had it since. The fat pine wood blacks the house so that the cook said she would not cook for us unless we would build a chimney, and today some of the men are building it.

Sunday Dec. the 19th. The week past I with two others pin[n]ed the pla[nks] on the forebay, and this morning I missed a basin and knife off from my shelf, stolen by some one. Home keeps running in my mind, and I feel somewhat lonesum especially Sundays, but my heart leaps with the expectation of geting home in the spring, and again it sometimes shrinks for fear that I will fail for want of means, but I keep up as good courage as I can.

Sunday Dec. the 26th. Last week I worked five days laid by yesterday, it being christmas. And to pass of the time I with 5 [others] went up on a mountain, on the other side of the American Fork to see the country around, and roll down rocks. And while there [we] could see the mountains around for some miles, some of them capt with snow. We also rolled down rocks, some of which would weigh a ton; they would go very fast, and sometimes jump some hundreds of feet and at last crash in the brush and and [sic] rocks below. When we arived at home we had bread and meat, and pumpkin and apple pies for dinner.

Sunday January the 2nd. 1848 Last week I have been at work and as Mr. Marshall has been gone about two weeks, we have rather hard times for the cook jeneraly puts the Beaf, and Bread, on the first table, and saves the pumpkin &c. for herself and the second table.

Tuesday Jan. the 11th. 1848 The past week I worked on the mill dam; and Sunday it began raining, and rained all day and night, and has rained off and on ever since. Today I worked half of the day in the rain.

Sunday Jan. the 16th. Haveing rained three days last week it raised the river very high, and we expected to see the water go around the butment almost every minute, but thursday the Sun came out and it has been clear ever since. The days are tolerable warm but the nights are very cold. Mr. Marshall has now been gone to the fort a month,[36] and has not came back yet, (with his mill irons) and Mr. Bennett has got very much out of patience waiting for him,[37] but we expect him all the time. Today I went down to the river and washed.

Sunday Jan. the 30th. 48 Mr. Marshall haveing arived we got liberty of him, and built a small house down by the mill, and last Sunday we moved into it in order to get rid of the brawling, partial, mistress, and cook for ourselves.[38] This week Mon. the 24th. [date inserted later] Mr. Marshall found some pieces of (as we all suppose) Gold, and he has gone to the Fort, for the Purpose of finding out.[39]

---

[36] Marshall on December 18, 1847, arrived at Sutter's Fort where he worked for some time in "making the Models for the Mill irons." On January 14, he and three others left the fort with the irons loaded in a wagon to return to the mill. See *New Helvetia Diary*, 101, 108.

[37] Charles Bennett was an energetic thirty-six-year-old builder and former First Dragoons soldier, hired about the same time as Smith and his companions, who apparently directed work on the mill in Marshall's absence. One of the earliest to travel west on the Oregon Trail, he was killed in 1855 near Walla Walla, Washington Territory, while serving as a captain of volunteers during the Yakima Indian War. See Rodman W. Paul, *The California Gold Discovery* (Georgetown, Calif.: Talisman Press, 1966), 28, 138–40, 145, 146.

[38] Her Mormon boarders at last threw off the imagined tyranny of Jennie Wimmer whose offense was put to rhyme by Henry Bigler:

"On Christmas morning in bed she swore

That she would cook for us no more

Unless we'd cum at the first call

For I am Mistress of you all."

[39] These lines and Henry Bigler's diary entry, "This day some kind of mettle was found in the tail race that that [sic] looks like goald," are the only eyewitness reports of the gold discovery made at the time. Although the exact date in Smith's handwriting was inserted later, the character of the two Mormons and the accuracy of their journals establish beyond reasonable doubt that the discovery occurred on January 24, 1848, and not five days before as later claimed by James Marshall. For more on this old controversy, see articles by John S. Hittell of the Society of California Pioneers in *Overland Monthly*, September 1887, and February 1888, and Rodman Paul, *California Gold Discovery*, 208–28.

An early sketch of the original Sutter's Mill showing in the foreground the tailrace where gold was discovered on January 24, 1848. Courtesy of California State Library, California Section.

It is found in the raceway in small pieces; some have been found that would weigh five dollars.

Sunday Febuary the 6th. Mr. Marshall has returned with the fact that it is Gold; and Captain Sutter came here wednesday with Johnston,[40] for the purpose of looking at the mine, where the Gold is found, and got enough for a ring.[41] The captain brought us a bottle of Liq-

---

[40] As this entry suggests, William Johnston, also phonetically spelled Johnstun, was not actually on the scene when gold was discovered, although he later claimed otherwise. Most evidence indicates the Ohioan had not yet returned from Sutter's Fort where he had gone for supplies.

[41] Sutter easily found some gold for himself because his Mormon hired hands had "salted" the millrace with some pieces of gold in the hope the master of New Helvetia would share with them some of the liquor he was known always to carry. See *Bigler's Chronicle*, 91–92.

uor, and some pocket knives. Thursday morning what should I find
on the shelf but my knife and basin haveing been brought by Johnstun and put there by him,[42] when we previously had asked him if
he knew any thing about it, and he afirmed that he did not. Still he
had hid it himself and kept it his untill the present time.

Monday Feb. the 14th. The past week I did not work but three
days and a half. Mr. Marshall grants us the privelege of picking up
Gold odd spells and Sundays,[43] and I have gathered up considerable.
When we shut down the gates the gold is found in the bottom
of the tale race.

Sunday Feb. the 20th. The fore part of the past week it rained
and I did not work but four days, and I have been drilling a rock
which is in the race, and blasting, which pleases the Indians very much
to see the rock which is very hard, split open so easy. Today I picked
up a little more of the root of all evil.[44]

Sunday March the 12th. The past two weeks, as usial, I have been
to work on the mill; and last Sunday I picked up two dollars and a
half, below this place about two miles. Today we started the mill,
and sawed up one log and are pining it on the forebay. The mill runs

---

[42] Smith obviously thought Johnston took the items, reported missing
on December 19, and restored them on February 2 when he returned to
the sawmill with Sutter. This would support other evidence that Johnston
was not actually on the scene the day of the discovery. Johnston later said
he did take part in the historic event, then went to the fort with Marshall
to report the find and came back with Sutter, but there is little to confirm
this story.

[43] In return, Smith and the other hired hands gave Marshall as much
as half of the gold they found. To secure their claim to the property, Sutter
and Marshall met with local Indian leaders soon after the discovery and
negotiated a three-year lease on a tract of land ten to twelve miles square
for some clothing, beads, trinkets, and colored handkerchiefs. See *Bigler's
Chronicle*, 92; also "Discovery of Gold at Coloma," *San Francisco Daily Herald*, December 31, 1855.

[44] Lacking mining know-how, the battalion veterans at this point ex-
tracted particles of gold from seams and crevices in the rocks with their pock-
etknives, a painfully slow process.

very well, but the back water hinders some, and the tale race will have to be dug some deeper.[45]

Sunday March the 19th. Last week we ran the mill some and it cuts well, makeing beautifull plank. Today I crossed the river and went down it to hunt for Gold, and found some. It has been raining most [of] the day. Brother Barger[46] came here this afternoon, from the Fort and sta[ted] that three wagons are on their way to this place with provision.

Tuesday March the 21st. Yesterday the wagons arived, with some Flour, Pumpkins, Pork &c. The wagons started on their way back today. [I] had a great notion of going with them to prepare for a start h[ome] but being requested by Marshall, I am a going to stay till the ne[xt] wagon comes which is to come in a few days.

Tuesday March the 28th. Last Sunday I with three others went [down] the river on the other side and picked up considerable Gold. Yest[erday] I recieved a letter from Father,[47] which pleases me much. He said that [he] arived at the Salt Lake, Oct the 27th. 1847. and had good luck except the loss of one horse. Mother is not there at present, but will be next Summer. Father wrote that provision was very scarce; corn is from six to seve[n] and wheat from nine, to ten

---

[45] It measures the integrity of the Mormon workmen that they resisted the temptation to look for gold and completed the project, but the sawmill within three months would be closed down anyway for the lack of personnel to operate it.

[46] Not much is known of William H. Barger, thirty-six, one of the Mormons at Sutter's Mill on January 24, 1848, other than he had lived at Nauvoo, enlisted as a private in the battalion's Company D, won promotion to corporal, and later resided for a time in Salt Lake City.

[47] This letter was probably delivered by a member of Jefferson Hunt's party which came to California over the southern route late in 1847 to obtain supplies for the new Mormon settlement in Salt Lake Valley. Also possible, but less likely, would be that it came by mounted express over the Truckee River trail, normally closed to wagons at this time of year. For more on Hunt's expedition, see Harold Schindler, *Orrin Porter Rockwell, Man of God, Son of Thunder* (Salt Lake City: University of Utah Press, 1966), 170–74.

dollars a bushel. He is a going to get some corn and wheat so that when the rest of the Family gets there we will have something to subsist upon.

Monday Appr 3d. Yesterday I with some others, again went down the river and picked up some more Gold.

Friday April the 7th. I have worked four days this week, but today I am laying by. Brot[hers] Brown, Stephens, and Bigler started today for the Fort,[48] but I thought that I would stay and work. Mr. Marshall has gave us the privelige [of] hunting Gold and haveing half we find, and we are a going [to take] the opportunity. I have something like thirty dollars of [gold].

Saturday April the 15th. The Boys have returned [from the] Fort and brought word that the first company are to start for Salt Lake today,[49] and the rest are to start on the first day of June, and I think that I Shall go down to the Fort and prepare for the trip.

As I have worked out one hundred dollars and upwards, besides what Gold I have picked up, I think that I shall be able to fit myself out, if I can get my pay, in things that I want, and at a reasonable price.

Sunday April the 23d. Last Monday I started from the Saw mill and arived here Tuesday; and I have been down to the Fort twice,

---

[48] Both North Carolinians and veterans of the battalion's Company D, thirty-three-year-old Alexander Stephens and his nephew, James Stephens Brown, nineteen, were among the six Mormon workers at Sutter's Mill when gold was discovered. Brown's version of the event, written years later and published in his autobiography, is useful, but less reliable than the contemporary accounts of Smith and Bigler. See James S. Brown, *Life of a Pioneer* (Salt Lake City: Geo. Q. Cannon & Sons Co., 1900).

[49] This apparently refers to Samuel Brannan's *California Star* express of ten men, most battalion veterans, who left Sutter's Fort the day of this entry to deliver by mule train some 2,000 copies of a special edition of Brannan's newspaper, announcing the gold discovery, as far east as the Missouri River and points between, including Salt Lake City. See *California Star*, San Francisco, April 1, 1848; Bailey, *Sam Brannan*, 122–24; *Bigler's Chronicle*, 106; *New Helvetia Diary*, 128; and Carroll D. Hall, ed., *The First Californian* (San Francisco: The Press of Lewis and Dorothy Allen, 1942), v–xi.

but I have not got any thing of Captain Sutter yet.[50] But today I went down to the store and bought a basin and some Sugar, to keep myself sweet. Two days of the past week I have been scraping on the Grist mill head race.

Sunday April the 30th. Since last week I have been down to the Fort three or four times, and have not recieved any thing towards a fit out for the journey home yet, except get[t]ing my saddle rig[g]ed, but I have any amount of promises, and I think I shall quit scraping, and be looking, for a fit out for HOME.

Friday May the 5th. Last Monday morning I started thinking that I would go up where the boys, some of them are gathering Gold. But not knowing the way, I took the wrong track and went about twenty miles up in the mountains and slep[t] under a pine tree, and it rained very hard all night.[51] The next day I started back and met the Company that were a going to explore the mountains to see if they could find a pass through them,[52] from here to the main emigration road, that leads to Salt Lake vall[e]y. And Brother Willis told me where the Gold mine was, (as near as he could,)[53] So I struck across to go to it, but it kept raining, and after travailing about twenty

---

[50] Though unable to pay his Mormon workers in cash, Sutter managed to settle up with them in livestock, clothing, wagons, seeds, tools, and other articles of value. He later prided himself that "there was not one of them who was not contented and satisfied." See J. A. Sutter, "The Discovery of Gold in California," *Hutchings' Illustrated California Magazine* 2 (November 1857): 194–98, reprinted in Paul, *California Gold Discovery*, 125–33.

[51] The place Smith sought was Mormon Island, a large sandbar in the South Fork of the American River, near present Folsom, where twenty-eight-year-old W. S. S. (Sidney) Willes and Wilford Hudson, twenty-nine, both battalion men, on March 2 made the first major gold strike after the Coloma discovery. At least seven Mormons were then using Indian baskets to wash out as much as $2 a load. The rich diggings became the destination of the 1849 gold rush.

[52] Chosen to find a new route over the mountains were Daniel Browett, Ira J. Willes, James C. Sly, Israel Evans, Jacob M. Truman, Ezra Allen, James R. Allred, Henderson Cox, and Robert Pixton.

[53] Ira Jones Willes was the thirty-six-year-old brother of Sidney Willes, discoverer of the rich Mormon Island placer diggings.

An exact copy of the first Sutter's Mill is this replica at Marshall Gold Discovery Historic State Park in Coloma on Highway 49 between Auburn and Placerville, some forty miles east of Sacramento.

miles that day, I again stoped under a tree, and it rained all night, and was very cold. And Wednesday, haveing nothing to eat, I again started for home and arived here in the afternoon about three oclock, being very tired. Yesterday I borrowed a horse and saddle, and went down to the Fort, and got a lariett and two sinches of the Captain and bought a pair of leggins of Weir[54] for three dollars.

Friday May the 26th. I scraped one day on the race, when on the nineth the boys came back from the exploring expedition have-ing went up to the back bones which was covered with Snow and they could not cross. They then concluded to go up to the Gold mine, so on Thursday the 11th. we went up, and stayed there untill Tuesday the 23d., when we came down.

While there we had very good luck; I got there something near three hundred dollars, which makes me in all some upwards of four hundred dollars. The most I made in a day was sixty five dollars af-ter the toll was taken out, which was thirty dollars out of a hundred, which goes to Hudson and Willis, that discovered the mine, and Bran-non who is securing it for them.[55] Before we came away, men, women and children, from the Bay and other places in California, were flock-ing to the gold mine, by the dozens, and by wagon loads.[56] While there Brannon called a me[e]ting, to see who was willing to pay toll

---

[54] Kentuckian Thomas Weir, forty-seven, had enrolled in the battalion as a corporal in Company A, but was discharged a private.

[55] Brannan was later accused of charging as much as thirty percent, or even a third, of the gold harvested by his Mormon Island brethren for tithing, taxes, and building a temple, but this entry indicates that Wilford Hudson and Sidney Willes each claimed a tenth for finding the placer and Brannan took the same share for undefined services to secure the property. The head of the *Brooklyn* Mormons was excommunicated in 1851, but not for extorting tithing gold or money from California church members. For details on Brannan, see "A Mormon Mission to California in 1851, from the Diary of Parley Parker Pratt," edited by Reva Holdaway Stanley and Charles L. Camp, *California Historical Quarterly* 14 (June 1935): 176.

[56] Within six weeks, Governor Richard B. Mason would find that vir-tually the entire male population of San Francisco had "gone to the mines." Elsewhere, he said, mills were abandoned, "houses vacant, and farms go-ing to waste." See Mason report, August 17, 1848, Exec. Doc. 17, H. R., 31st Cong., 1st sess., 1850.

and who was not. The most of them agreed to pay toll, but some of them would not.[57] Agreeable to the council of brothers Rogers, Browett, and Holmes, I with Douglass, Dobson, Dennett, Moss and Rogers came down to finish the race, and fit ourselves out for going to Salt Lake vally by the middle of June.[58] Some of the boys came here last night that have been geting Gold on the other side of the river.[59]

Tuesday May the 30th. Today I went down to the Fort which is the third or fourth time since I came from the mine and have not got any animals of the Captain yet. But last week I bought a horse for the money, (as I want to get things ready to start by the middle of June,) and gave seventy dollars for him.

Saturday June the 3d. Yesterday I went down to the Fort and got an order on Smith, (a storekeeper)[60] from the captain and bought

---

[57] When one of the dissenters asked Mason, who visited Mormon Island on July 5, what right Brannan had to collect the toll, he was told the promoter had every right "if you Mormons are fool enough to pay it." See William T. Sherman, *Memoirs*, 2 vols., 4th ed. (New York: C. W. Webster, 1892), 1:53.

[58] Smith and several others apparently went back to work on the race for the gristmill because the Mormons feared Sutter might not pay them for work already done if the job was not finished. Three of those named, Daniel Browett, thirty-eight, Joseph Dobson, forty-two, and David H. Moss, twenty-nine, were Englishmen. The others were Samuel H. Rogers, twenty-nine, Ohio; Jonathan H. Holmes, forty-two, Massachusetts; Daniel Q. Dennett, forty, Maine; and James Douglas, about twenty-five, birthplace unknown.

[59] They probably included forty-five-year-old Benjamin Hawkins from New York and Ohioan Marcus Lafayette Shepherd, twenty-three, discoverers of the rich placer, later named Negro Bar, across the American River's South Fork from Mormon Island.

[60] The storekeeper was the same Charles Smith who rode east with Brannan in 1847 to meet Brigham Young's pioneer company, then carried to California the news the Mormon destination was Salt Lake Valley. Afterward, he became Brannan's partner in a store at Sutter's Fort, operated at the time referred to here under the name C. C. Smith and Company. He later sold out for $50,000 to Brannan who renamed the venture S. Brannan & Company and positioned himself to make a fortune from the gold rush.

a bolt of hickry shirting, 25 lbs of sug[ar] &c. to the amount of twenty two dollars.

Wednesday June the 7th. The boys jenerally are prepareing for the t[rip] to Salt Lake, but there are some a going to stay till fall. A great many have came from the bay also to fit themselves out. I have been down to the Fort again today, to see if I could get a mule of the Captain, and he promised me that he would have one for me by next Saturday. Brother Weir within a day or two has gone crazy and is all the time busy talking, walking and preaching about some[thing].[61]

Friday, June the 9th. Yesterday I went down to the Fort and boug[ht] some Flour. This morning I heard that there was a man drowned at the mines, by undertaking to cross the river on a small craft and was taken down over the rapids, and the boat broke, and the man could not Swim, but drowned.

Monday June the 12th. Last Saturday I went down to the Fort to traid some out of the store and get my mule, but the Captain hated to let the mule go out of [the] mill and wanted I should take a good horse, and a Jackass. And [I] told him that I would be down Sunday and see, if the animals were jentle to suit me perhaps I would take them.

We got an order on Smiths store, and I traided something l[ike] thirdy five dollars, of clothing. Sunday I went down to the Fort again, but the captain was in rather of a poor humor and said it was Sunday and I could not get any animals. While there a man came and claimed my horse and swore that he would die before he would let it go from there, but the bystanders and some of the Boys said he could not take the horse without proving that it was his, and told me to get on my horse when I pleased. And I being ready jumped on my horse and came off.

Today I again went down bound to get a mule of the Capt if possible, and I happened to catch him in a good humor, and he turned

---

[61] This disorder proved temporary because Thomas Weir went on later that year to Utah where he settled at Logan and died one day short of his seventy-fifth birthday.

one of his Mill Mules over to me. I then went to the store, and bought a pair of buckskin pants $.6. and a pamets hat $.8.,00 and a bottle of Jin $1.50, for medicine.[62]

Sunday June the 18th. The past week I have been byeing Clothing &c. to take Home to the amount of forty two dollars; and have $.160. left.

Wednesday June the 21st. Yesterday the Cariard,[63] (or band of horses) started for the mountains, and I was at a loss whether to go or not as I had been calculating to pack my mules, but David Moss, which owned a wagon in partnership with Rogers and Dobson, which were sick and concluded to wait till fall and go up to Mr. Thomkins,es this Summer untill they get well and Brother Rogers is to take Brother Moss,es things through to Salt Lake Vally, and as he wants help I think of going with him.[64] I have two Mules, two Horses and one Mare which I think will easyly take me to Salt Lake Vally whether I go in a wagon or not.

Thursday June the 22nd. Yesterday I went down to the Fort and bought some things to the amount of fourteen dollars, part of which went to Brother Rogers to pay for a share of a barrel part full of potatoes, which cost twenty five dollars. The reason why we bought the

---

[62] From such modest purchases, incoming gold seekers made sales boom at Brannan's stores where daily receipts by October did "not fall much short of $3,000, of which $2,000 are clear profit over & above all expenses," estimated Lieutenant William T. Sherman. See *The California Gold Fields in 1848, Two Letters from Lt. W. T. Sherman, U. S. A.* (privately printed for Frederick W. Beinecke, Christmas, 1964).

[63] One of many forms of the Spanish word, *caballada*, then used for drove of horses. Animals of those going to Salt Lake Valley were driven to an assembly point in the foothills where Henry Bigler and two companions built a corral and named the place Pleasant Valley. Still so named, the location is about eight miles southeast of present Placerville.

[64] For whatever reason, Moss and Dobson eventually changed their minds and went with Smith's company to Salt Lake Valley rather than stay for a time with Thomas Tompkins and his family. Tompkins, his wife, and two children had come to California in 1846 with Brannan on the *Brooklyn* and located in the vicinity of Sutter's Fort.

potatoes at so high a price, was because there is a complaint out, which some call the dry land scurvy, and they say that the potatoes will cure it. And we thought that we would try it.

This complaint first commences in the Knees and turns them purple, and makes one very Sick, and lame, this is the Sickness that Dobsond and Moss is troubled with.

I have been some lame with it, but I am geting better now.

We expected to start today, for the mountains, but Rogers went to Sanclairs, to get some cows,[65] and did not get back in time and we expect to start tomorrow.

---

[65] John Sinclair, an associate of Sutter, was probably not at his home on the American River's right bank, about three miles above Sutter's Fort, when Rogers called because the hard-drinking Scotsman with some fifty Indian laborers was washing for gold with closely woven willow baskets on the American River's North Fork "with good success," according to H. H. Bancroft, *History of California* (San Francisco: History Company, Publishers, 1888), 6:73.

5

TRAIL TO EL DORADO
June 25–September 29, 1848

For California, where James Marshall found gold on January 24, the year 1848 would be the year before the flood. Within two weeks of the discovery at Sutter's Mill, dominion over the land passed from Mexico to the United States under a treaty that gave James Polk all he wanted for less than $20 million. Time was running out for an idyllic way of life in a sun-blessed region, protected from intrusion over land by the lofty Sierra Nevada and from the sea by the joined continents of the western hemisphere.

As yet unaware of the momentous events at Coloma, most westering Americans that year, to their later regret, would play it safe at Fort Hall and decide in favor of Oregon. Only a hundred or so covered wagons would roll over the trail to California to bring not many more than 400 stout spirits,[1] undaunted by the War with Mexico or the tragedy which had befallen the Donner party during the winter of 1846–47.

But the dam was about to burst, the outside world to pour in, and the peaceful country of Spanish missions, vast cattle ranches, and matchless horsemen after 1848 would be forever changed. Within ten years, the *Mountain Democrat*, for example, one of three newspapers serving the new mining town of Placerville, would devote twenty-three full columns in four consecutive issues just to list local citizens who were delinquent on their taxes.

As news of the gold discovery spread, untold thousands braced themselves to risk life itself to reach the placer diggings at Mormon

---

[1] For more on the 1848 immigration, see George R. Stewart, *The California Trail* (New York: McGraw-Hill Book Co., 1962), 193–216.

Island and Negro Bar on the South Fork of the American River. From across the United States, where a mass movement west was about to begin, and from all parts of the world, they would come by every conceivable route and mode of transportation.[2]

Still, not every heart pounded that year with the desire to go to California. Azariah Smith was already there, right at the very place they all yearned to be, and all he wanted was to leave and go home.

"At the time Marshall discovered gold at the saw mill, I was ill," he told the *San Francisco Examiner* on the fiftieth anniversary of the gold discovery. "The news that glistening gold was all around did not make me as enthusiastic as it might have had I been well."

"I was home-sick as well as physically sick," he confessed. "I wanted to see my mother and I did not care whether there was gold in the locality or not."[3]

So it was that the young Mormon joined a company of coreligionists, mainly battalion veterans and former followers of Samuel Brannan, who assembled in the foothills some fifty miles east of Sutter's Fort for the journey to the new gathering place of their faith in Salt Lake Valley. Impatient at every delay, he collected his resources, including a small hoard of nuggets, and prepared to go to a home he had never seen, to be with his mother. But this was not yet the end of Azariah Smith's involvement in the significant events of 1846–48 which would shape the future of California and the American west.

To avoid the more than two dozen crossings of the Truckee River on the established California Trail to the north of Lake Tahoe, opened by wagons in 1844, Smith's company undertook to pioneer a new route over the Sierra Nevada, some fifty miles to the south. Following the divide between the American and Cosumnes rivers, they would push their seventeen wagons and two small cannons over the mountains at Kit Carson Pass on the south side of the lake.

The route they opened that summer, now known as the Mormon-Carson Pass Emigrant Trail, would become a great highway to the goldfields—a trail to El Dorado—for tens of thousands of gold rushers

---

[2] One of the best of many books is J. S. Holliday, *The World Rushed In, The California Gold Rush Experience, An Eyewitness Account of a Nation Heading West* (New York: Simon and Schuster, 1981). Also see Donald Dale Jackson, *Gold Dust* (New York: Knopf, 1980).

[3] *San Francisco Examiner*, January 24, 1898.

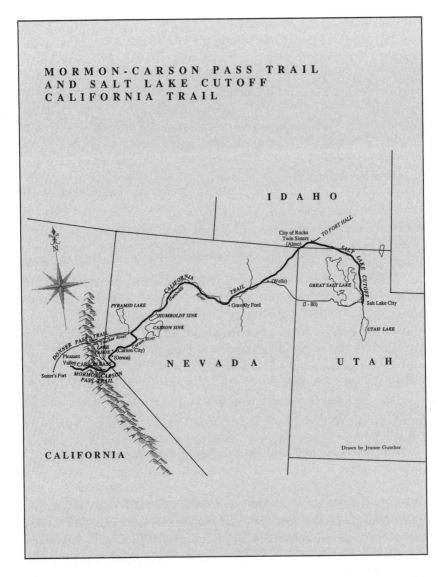

over the years to come. More than 6,000 emigrants would cross the
Sierra Nevada by the new trail in 1849 alone.[4]

---

[4] Thomas H. Hunt of Palo Alto, Calif., has identified the exact route
of the Mormon-Carson Pass Emigrant Trail which has been marked by
Trails West, Inc. Other authorities on the early road include Ben Lofgren
of Sacramento and Thomas Mahach of Pollock Pines, Calif.

On rejoining the established trail east of the mountains, Smith and his comrades would meet along the Humboldt River most of the emigrant wagons journeying to California in 1848, few in number, but led by such captains as James Clyman and Joseph Chiles, whose owners had not heard of the gold discovery before leaving the Missouri River. Most of these trains would follow the tracks made by Smith's eastbound company and thus become the first wagons to cross the Sierra Nevada by the new route, going west.[5]

The reaction of these weary emigrants when the Mormons displayed the contents of their leather pouches can only be imagined. According to a member of Smith's party, one old fellow, estimated to be more than seventy in years, "sprang to his feet, threw his old wool hat upon the ground and jumped upon it with both feet, then kicked it high in the air, and exclaimed, 'Glory hallalujah, thank God, I shall die a rich man yet!' "[6]

Whether he did or not, Azariah Smith was never to doubt where the true treasures of life were to be found. When asked in 1898, fifty years later, if he had ever been sorry he left California when those who stayed behind were harvesting gold valued at $700 or more in a single day, he responded without hesitation.

"I have never regretted leaving the mines," he said, and "never wished myself back there."

"If I had stayed there I would have been under the ground in a short time. By coming away I have lived to be sixty-nine years of age."[7]

And when he said that he still had nearly fifteen years to go.

[The Journal]

Sunday June the 25th. We did not get started Friday or Saturday, neither are we to start today, but tomorrow I think we will get started. Some of the wagons have to go up to the mine to get the tire

---

[5] See Charles L. Camp., ed., *James Clyman, Frontiersman, The Adventures of a Trapper and Covered-Wagon Emigrant As Told in His Own Reminiscences and Diaries* (Portland, Oreg.: Champoeg Press, 1960) and Helen S. Giffen, *Trail-Blazing Pioneer, Colonel Joseph Ballinger Chiles* (San Francisco: John Howell-Books, 1969).

[6] Tyler, *Concise History*, 340.

[7] *San Francisco Examiner*, January 24, 1898.

set,[8] before they will do to cross the mountains. Two of the Boys came down from the camp, (where they are camping to prepare for a start over the Mountains,) and said that they had good luck going to that place. The distance is about fifty miles.[9]

Wednesday July the 5th. A week ago last Monday we started; and part of the wagons went up to the Mine and got the tire set on their wagons, and I went, with the remainder of the wagons on up to the camp helping drive the cows, and loose cattle; and on Wednesday we arived there. But the wagons that went to the mine, did not get to the camp untill Saturday. Brother Daniel Browett, Ezra H Allen & Henderson Cox have gone on over the Mountains, to find the best pass,[10] and have not got back yet. There is a man here that is a going to pack over the mountains to Salt Lake vally, and I calculate to acompany him.[11] On Monday [July 3] we packed up and travailed something like twenty five miles when we came up with some of the wagons that started a day or two ago, and by going about two miles off from the wagons, we came to a vally and good feed for our animals, where we built a Carell,[12] and [this] morning some of the

---

[8] To save money, company members did their own blacksmithing at the Mormon Island diggings, near present Folsom, rather than pay for such work at Sutter's Fort.

[9] This is a good estimate of the trail distance from Sutter's Fort to the assembly camp for the emigration party at Pleasant Valley in the Sierra Nevada foothills, near present Placerville.

[10] First names of the three were inserted in Smith's handwriting at a later date. Browett, a thirty-eight-year-old Englishman, was a natural leader who had served as a sergeant in the battalion's Company E; Allen, thirty-three, came from New York; and Cox, an Indiana native, had joined the battalion two years before at age sixteen.

[11] Smith and his partner were among a party of forty-five men and one woman who left Pleasant Valley on July 2 to make the Sierra Nevada crossing. They would be overtaken by as many as twenty-one others on the trail. For the best source on the makeup of this company, see Norma Baldwin Ricketts, *Tragedy Spring and the Pouch of Gold* (Sacramento: Ricketts Publishing Co., 1983).

[12] They called this valley Sly Park in honor of its finder, forty-year-old James C. Sly of New York, a Company B veteran, who died seventeen years later at Levan, Utah. Still so named, it is located today on El Dorado County Road E16.

Boys went ahead to see what had become [of] the others,[13] and we expect to camp here till they return.

Monday July the 10th. We are still laying by a waiting for [those] that went ahead to come back. Last Saturday Mr. Perke came h[ere] for the purpose of taking the mans horse, (or pony) that is pack[ing] with me, but he would not let it go, so Perke started for Saint Clairs to get a writ for him,[14] but I think that he might as wel[l] mind his business. Some of the Boys, (or men) came down today [and] built a carell for the cattle, as they begin to wander off rather fa[st] through the night.

Wednesday July the 12th. Yesterday the Men came down from the camp and built another Carell for the horses, as the other is not large enough.

Friday July the 14th. Yesterday I went to the camp and they all ag[reed] to be cheerfull, and are waiting with anxiety for those to come back that went ahead. And this morning two of them came down here t[o] bring their horses. They stated that they had been in sight of [the] vally on the other side of the Mountains, finding a very [good] pass.[15] But they did not see any thing of the three that went [first].

Saturday July the 15th. This morning some of the Boys from [the] camp came down here for the purpose of yokeing up the [oxen] and driving them with the cows up to the camp in [front]. There are three or four going ahead to cut the brush, and throw the stones out of

---

[13] A party of ten was sent to search for Browett, Allen, and Cox, who had set out on June 25 to find the best route over the mountains.

[14] The unwelcome visitor was probably John D. Perkey from Sutter's Fort whose attempt to claim the horse would undoubtedly be frustrated by the fact that John Sinclair, alcalde for the Sacramento District, at that time was on a fork of the American River washing gold. Perkey entered Sutter's service in 1845 when he came from Oregon in the McMahon party. See Hubert H. Bancroft, *California Pioneer Register and Index, 1542-1848* (Baltimore: Regional Publishing Co., 1964), 282.

[15] After crossing two summits and reaching the headwaters of the Carson River, which empties into the Great Basin, this party had spent six days in an unsuccessful search for a better route.

the way.[16] The horses are a going to stay a few days and let the teams go ahead, and I do not know whether I shall start today or not.

Tuesday July the 18th. 1848 Haveing waited till Monday, I then started with Mr. Diamond,[17] (the man that is packing with me) after the horses; and my mules went ahead, and got with the horses, and bothered me very much.

After travailing about twenty five miles, we came to a little vally where the wagons had encamped.[18] Some of the Men have gone ahead today, to clear the way, and the wagons will start tomorrow, and I am a going to start to[o]. This morning I and Mr. Diamond went a hunting, but did not see any game. Some of the Boys also went back this morning to find some cows, and horses that were left yesterday, and they found them all but one or two. This afternoon those men that went ahead, saw some Indians, with clothing on which resembled those of Brothers Browett, Allen and Cox. They also saw a place where they suspect that they are killed and buried.[19]

Thursday July the 20th. Yesterday we travailed about eight miles when we came to the place where the Brethren were supposed to have

---

[16] The road-clearing party included Henry Bigler, Francis Hammond, converted to Mormonism at San Francisco by members of the *Brooklyn* company, and two others, unidentified.

[17] The only non-Mormon member of the company, twenty-five-year-old James Diamond joined the faith soon after his arrival in Utah where he was among the first settlers of Manti in 1849. A native of Kerry County, Ireland, Diamond in 1847 had traveled overland to Oregon, then sailed to San Francisco on the ship *Henry*. He later settled at Springville, Utah, where he died in 1908. See Frank Esshom, *Pioneers and Prominent Men of Utah* (Salt Lake City: Western Epics, Inc., 1966), 120. Other information was provided by Flora Diamond of Springville, Utah.

[18] They called this camp Leek Springs after liliaceous plants, resembling wild onions, found there in abundance. Still so named, it is located on the Mormon Emigrant Trail Road, near the junction of State Highway 88, in El Dorado County.

[19] As the road-clearing party was returning to the Leek Springs camp, it "found the place where we supposed our three pioneers had camped by a large spring," Bigler said. "Near where they had their fire, was the appearance of a fresh grave." See *Bigler's Chronicle*, 114.

At Tragedy Springs, rocks placed by Azariah Smith and others still mark the grave of three comrades, Daniel Browett, Ezra Allen, and Henderson Cox, who were "supposed to have been Murdered and Buried by Indians" on the Mormon-Carson Pass Emigrant Trail.

been killed and thrown into that hole, and covered with dirt by the Indians.[20] After examining till we were sure that they were all three there, we again covered them up, and searched to see what we could discover, and found Brother Allens purse with some upwards of a hundred dollars in it.[21] The manner in which they were supposed to have been overcome, and killed, were thus. They were supposed to have stoped there to camp for the night and some Indians came, and in a friendly way stayed with them; and the Brethren not thinking that they were thus cruel, was not attall afraid of them, as they had been working a great deal in the Mountains, with them through the winter. Thus not suspecting them, they all layed down, as they supposed in safety [and] after they had got fast asleep, a body of Indians crept up on them from behind the rocks, which were thick, and poured a heavy shower of arrows on them, and before they could gather their arms, in time to defend themselves against their enemies they were killed on the spot. From the appearance of things Brother Allen got his six shooter, and got behind a big rock to protect himself. But there being so many Indians, they rushed upon him and mashed him in pieces with rocks, where the purse was found, which was covered with blood. There were a great many arrows also picked up which were covered with blood. The company was then organised in four tens, and Brother Thompson was apointed Captain;[22] and in the evening,

---

[20] Comrades of the slain men named this place Tragedy Springs, an affluent of the Cosumnes River, found today on State Highway 88 at the crossing of the Carson Emigrant Trail about four miles east of the Mormon Emigrant Trail junction and thirteen miles west of Kit Carson Pass. Browett's family, including his wife, parents, and a brother and sister, arrived in Salt Lake that fall. Allen's wife, Sarah, later settled with their two children in Utah where she remarried. The parents of young Cox reached Salt Lake Valley shortly before Smith's company arrived in September.

[21] The pouch of gold, worn on a string around his neck, was delivered to Allen's wife by Wilford Hudson. From some of the nuggets she had fashioned a wedding ring that she wore for the rest of her life. See Ricketts, *Tragedy Spring*, 30–31.

[22] An experienced officer, thirty-five-year-old Samuel Thompson of New York had led a battalion force that killed six Indians near Los Angeles a year before in the only hostile action carried out by the Mormon command. The former second lieutenant of Company E later settled at Spanish Fork, Utah.

after fireing the cannon which started the horses running, and some of them ran off.[23] Three of the tens then went through the timber in different directions to see if there was any Indians about, and drive the horses and cattle together while the other ten stayed and guarded camp. In the morning fifteen of the men went after the horses, and those that stayed built a wall around the place where the Brethren were buried, and filled it up level with stone inside. And on a tree close by was engraven by Hudson.

Sacred to the Memory of Daniel Browett, Ezrah H. Allen, and Henderson Cox. Who was supposed to have been murdered and buried, by the Indians on the night of the 27th. of June 1848.[24]

On the twentyeth, we built a carell for the horses to keep them from running off again through the night; and some of the Boys came with part of the horses which had been driven around [by] the Indians, but they could not drive them off, and their [tracks] were thick all over the old camping ground, where the horses [were].

Saturday July the 22nd. Yesterday morning, some of the Boys went after horses, there being some fifty missing yet, and they found them all, but three, which haveing trail ropes on I suppose that [the] Indians have caught them. One of them was Mr. Diamonds pack Mule; and he with two others went back to see if they could find [them]

---

[23] To frighten any prowling Indians away, Thompson ordered the company to "limber up" one of the two small field pieces the Mormons had purchased more than two months before from John Sutter and "let her speak once." If the report alarmed the natives, it made an even greater impression on the party's livestock which scattered in all directions as far as twenty-five miles. Sutter had acquired the bronze cannons, a four and a six pounder, from the Russians at Fort Ross on the northern California coast. See Tyler, *Concise History*, 338, and *Bigler's Chronicle*, 116.

[24] To clear a place for these words, Wilford Hudson chopped away the bark on one side of a large pine near the grave. In 1929, the tree fell, breaking off about six feet above the inscription. To preserve the memorial, the stump was cut two years later and moved to the Marshall Gold Discovery Historic State Park museum at Coloma where it was restored in 1988. The stones placed by Smith and his comrades still mark the grave which is preserved at a roadside park, dedicated in 1967 by Daughters of Utah Pioneers, Sacramento County; Sons of Utah Pioneers, Sierra Chapter; Explorer Scout units; and the U.S. Forest Service.

The tip of a gnarled pine, foreground, points to the notch in the Sierra Nevadas where Azariah Smith's Mormon party opened the trail over West Pass, at more than 9,600 feet above sea level the highest point in the United States crossed by covered wagons.

and while they were gone, the wagons started, and we packed Diamonds things on one of the Boys mules, and started; and after a little the [three] came, but did not find the animals. After travailing about four [miles] to Rock Valley we encamped and built another Carell. This evening [one name lost from torn page] Hudson, and Thompson, killed a Deer. Saturday morning some [of] the men went ahead to clear out the road.

Tuesday July the 25th. Sunday some of the Boys again went ahead to fix the road, and Monday we started, and travailed about Seven miles, haveing a very bad road, for the wagons; and Brother Rogers wagon tip[p]ed over twice; and several wagons got broke, and today they [are] fixing them, and geting the remainder of them to camp.[25]

Wednesday July the 26th. Today I packed my mules and [traveled] with Brother Corays pack horses. I have not got my packs [and] packsaddles fixed so that I think my packs will ride [better] and my Mules are jentle. We went about two miles down the Canion, to frozen Lake, and encamped, in Lake Vally,[26] with the best of feed. There is a great many, Lakes through the Mountains which are Small. There is also some Snow on the sides of the Mountains part of which we travailed over. This afternoon there has ten men started to explore the road on ahead, and we do not expect them back till tomorrow night.

Saturday July the 29th. 48 Last Thursday, I with fourteen others went ahead and made road. And in the evening the Boys came back, that went to find the best pass, without makeing any farther discovery. Friday we moved our camp within a quarter of a mile, of the back bone, it being six miles, and encamped, in a small vally, and it is called Summit camp, because it is the highest that we expect to camp. Today the wagons are crossing the back bone,[27] and going down

---

[25] Broken or not in the effort, the wagons were the first to cross West Pass, highest of two summits on the Mormon-Carson Pass Emigrant Trail, between Silver Lake and Caples Lake on Highway 88. At more than 9,600 feet above sea level, the pass is also the highest point crossed by covered wagons in the United States. See Jeanne H. Watson, ''The Carson Emigrant Road,'' *Overland Journal*, Oregon-California Trails Association, 4 (Summer 1986): 4–12.

[26] This camping place, then on a meadow near two small lakes, is now probably under the waters of Caples Lake, one larger body formed by a later dam and named after the early owner of a nearby ranch. Between Tragedy Springs and the lake, the trail opened by the Mormon party ran to the south of Silver Lake and Highway 88.

[27] The second of the summits on the route over the Sierra Nevada was crossed at the 8,600-foot Kit Carson Pass on today's Highway 88, named for the famous scout who guided Frémont and his expedition over the range

the Mountain on the other side which is very steep, and the men have to hold the wagons to keep them from tip[p]ing over.

Monday July the 31st. On Saturday, the wagons got down the back bone, and travailed two miles, (in all) and encamped by, Red Lake, with two wagons broke. They mended them, and Sunday we travailed about five miles, down Hope Vally,[28] haveing a good road (considering the mountains,) and encamped at the head of a canion, that we expect to pass through about fifteen miles long, called pass canion. There is also a river runs through the canion, which is called pass River, in which some of the Boys have caught Trout. Last night we killed four mountain Chickens, and two ducks, and this morning we had a fine pot pie. Some of the Boys have been ahead to fix the road, today and they say it is very bad, and seemingly impos[s]ible for the wagons to get through. Today I made a pair of pantaloons.

Wednesday August the 2nd. Yesterday I went with some twenty others, to fix the road in the canion, and it is indeed very bad, and hundreds, and hundreds of feet up either side.[29] We did not get the road finished, and there has some more men gone today to finish it.

Friday August the 4th. 48 Yesterday some more men went to work in the canion.

This morning I took my Mules and packed them for Strong[30] and Dennett; and while on the way, in the canion, at the first crossing of the river, which was very bad, one of my Mules lamed itself very bad, on one of the rocks. After taking the load through the canion,

---

in 1844. The pass is a true divide in that it separates the waters of the Pacific slope and the Great Basin.

[28] This name was given because the company here began "to have hope" they would make the mountain crossing. The valley still bears the name. See *Bigler's Chronicle*, 118.

[29] Later emigrants would consider the six-mile Carson Canyon on the Carson River's West Fork one of the worst stretches on the entire overland trail to California. The route from Kit Carson Pass through the canyon is followed closely today by Highway 88.

[30] A Company E veteran, twenty-year-old William Strong appropriately hailed from a western Pennsylvania hamlet named Strongstown.

I went back, and got my load, with one mule, by packing one horse. The distance was about five miles.

Saturday August the 5th. We did not start till noon waiting for some of the men to kill a beaf, but the wagons went ahead. There has fourteen more men caught up with us today, haveing came from Pleasant Vally in five days. We travailed twelve miles when we came up with the wagons, and encamped.[31]

Sunday August the 6th. 48 I put my things in Douglass,es wagon and help drive the horses; we travailed about twenty miles; and in the evening the mountains was fairly covere[d] with fires, at Indians camps, and a good many of them came in camp.[32]

Monday August the 7th. I packed my Mules, and we travailed twenty miles, and encamped on pilot River haveing followed it down from the Mountains.[33] This morning the Buckaroes missed two or three horses and tracked them about five miles, but did not get them as they had no arms with them, and was afraid of the Indians as their tracks were thick.

Wednesday August the 9th. Yesterday we travailed eleven miles, and encamped on Pilot River. The pack Company went ahead. To-day we travailed fifteen miles. Nights we make a carell of our wagons, to put the horses in, and have a guard to guard them, and the cattle. Today my things was in the wagon.

Thursday August the 10th. 48 We layed by [in] order to hunt some animals that were stolen, by the Indians through the night, and

---

[31] This pack party started nearly a month behind but without wagons caught up quickly over a now-improved trail. Bigler said it numbered thirteen and came up on August 3. All camped about four miles south of the hot springs on today's Nevada Route 206.

[32] After passing through present Genoa [Mormon Station], they came to the bend in the river where they made the Rattlesnake Camp, named after the rattler killed there, about two miles east of present Carson City on the line of U.S. Highway 50.

[33] They actually followed the Carson River. The name Pilot was one of but few the Mormon trail makers bestowed that failed to endure.

The guns of old Fort Churchill, established in 1860, still overlook the emigrant road along the Carson River in western Nevada, opened by Smith and his companions a dozen years before.

found them all but one, which was bro[ther] Pickups.[34] They found one of them in the brush; the Indians [were] persued to[o] close, cut the rope that was on his neck and hobb[led] him with it. They saw

---

[34] George Pickup, twenty-seven, was a native of Manchester, England, and a former private in the battalion's Company C.

plenty of Indian tracks, and some Ind[ians], one of which sculking towards the river, they hurried up to him [and] gave him a shot. After a little he turned and shot four arrows at Mr Diamond, one of which hit him in the breas[t] [but] did not injure him much. And in the evening when the [cattle] drove in, one of the calves was badly wounded, haveing been [shot] by the Indians. This camp ground was named Oxbow Camp ground.[35]

Friday August the 11th. Last night I was on guard; [and] today we travailed eleven miles.

Sunday August the 13th. Yesterday we left pilot River at the packers camp,[36] and travailed twenty five miles in a north west direction, when we came to Trucky river, where the road [crosses] and goes over to the Sink of Maries river.[37] Last night [I was] on guard.

Tuesday August the 15th. Ye[sterday mor]ning we left Trucky river and travailed twenty five mil[es] [when] we came to the hot

---

[35] The Ox Bow camp on Carson River was located near the later site of Fort Churchill, established in 1860 to protect emigrants against Indian attack, now preserved as a Nevada State Historic Park, eight miles south of present Silver Springs, Nev., on Alt. U.S. Highway 95. Smith's entries, including distances covered each day, indicate the company traveled by the route now known as the Fort Churchill Road, which generally follows the Carson River between today's Dayton, Nev., and Fort Churchill.

[36] According to Trails West, which has mapped their route, they left the Carson River about three miles east of Silver Springs, near today's Lahontan Dam, and moved northward on the line of Alt. U.S. Highway 95 to meet the established California Trail at present Wadsworth, Nev., where the Truckee River turns sharply north toward Pyramid Lake. But the distance and direction given by both Smith and Bigler suggest that their trail may have followed more closely the line of present Alt. U.S. Highway 50 to its junction with Interstate 80. See Thomas H. Hunt, *The California Trail*, Fourth Annual National Convention, Oregon-California Trails Association, Carson City, Nevada, August 20–24, 1986, Map #3. Also see *Bigler's Chronicle*, 120.

[37] The stretch between the Truckee River at present Wadsworth and the sink of the Humboldt River, called Mary's River by early trappers, was known to later emigrants as the Forty-Mile Desert, a dreaded *jornada* without grass or water, except for a sulfurous hot spring about midway.

springs, there being no water or [wood but] what we brought with us. The spring was so hot [we made] coffee by puting the water in a kettle with the coffee, and placing it in the spring, it soon made coffee.[38] We carelled the horses, and guarded the cattle, till eleven oclock giveing them a little water and grass which we brought with us, and then hitched up and started; and I with some others got through to a Slough of brackish water a lit[t]le after Sunrise, on the 15th) and after a lit[t]le the wagons and cattle rolled in.[39] The distance is about twenty two miles. It is a hot day, and the Boys mostly are laying under the wagons in the shade a sleeping, as we did not get to sleep much last night.

Wednesday August the 16th. In the after noon yesterday, some sixteen wagons came in, on the way to California, from the States, and they got a waybill of us—calculating to take our trail over the mountains.[40] Last Night I was on guard, and today we met another

----

[38] According to Bigler, it also "scalded to death and boiled to pieces" a little dog that fell in. The boiling spring can be seen today at the Hot Springs-Nightingale Exit 65 on Interstate 80 in western Nevada where Geothermal Food Processors uses the heat from its waters to dehydrate onions.

[39] Since men and animals were relatively fresh, the Mormon company arrived at the sink of the Humboldt River, some seven miles west of present Lovelock, Nev., without reported loss in livestock or equipment. But the Forty-Mile Desert would later take a fearful toll on westbound teams and wagons, already worn down by months of travel.

[40] This would be the train led by the noted frontiersman James Clyman, then fifty-six, who had come west as early as 1823 with William Ashley. The Virginian's company counted some disaffected Mormons from Salt Lake Valley, including thirty-six-year-old Hazen Kimball from New Hampshire, his wife, Decinda, twenty-nine, and two children, Helen, six, and George, four, both born in Hancock County, Ill., a man named Rogers, and possibly other Utah pioneers of 1847. Kimball had served as a captain of 10 in the company of 100 led by Jedediah M. Grant, later counselor to Brigham Young, which arrived in Salt Lake Valley on October 2, 1847. The only Rogers listed in the immigration that year was Isaac Rogers from Connecticut. Clyman did follow the new road, opened by Smith's party, to make his wagons first to cross the Sierra Nevada on the Carson River route, going west. See *Bigler's Chronicle*, 121; Camp, *James Clyman, Frontiersman*, 237; J. Roderick Korns, "West from Fort Bridger," *Utah Historical Quarterly* 19 (1951): 260–61; and Carter, *Heart Throbs*, 8:401–48, which lists Utah pioneers of 1847 as confirmed by the L.D.S. Church Historian's Office.

train of wagons, on the road to California.[41] We travailed 20 miles & encamped.

Friday August the 18th. Yesterday we travailed fifteen miles and encamped on Maries River and in the evening three Indians came in camp; and when we carelled the horses one of them was wounded on the wether, by an Indian arrow, and we kept the Indians under guard through the night, and I was one of the guard. Today we travailed ten miles, with my mind longing for home, we encamped with scarcely any feed for our animals.

Sunday Aug the 20th. Yesterday morning brother Browetts cow, being so lame that she could not travail, we killed her and divided her out to the company. We travailed fifteen miles, and encamped, with midling good feed; and we had not been in camp long, before two horses were shot, with Indian arrows, one on the back, and the other on the fore leg.[42] Then, some of the men went out to watch, for the Indians, and shot at two. But they did not know whether they hit or not, as they were in the bushes. Today we are laying by.

Monday August the 21st. Today we travailed thirty miles, and did not get camped till after dark.

Tuesday August the 22nd. We travailed twenty miles.

Wednesday August the 23d. We also travailed twenty miles; there has been several animals left lately being shot by the Indians.

---

[41] These wagons, some twenty-five in number, may have belonged to the company with twenty-six-year-old Pierre Barlow Cornwall whose seven-man pack party had joined a larger wagon outfit for protection from Indians. The Cornwall train also followed the tracks of Smith's company to California where the New Yorker became a leading industrialist and politician. See Stewart, *California Trail*, 201.

[42] Known as "Diggers," the Great Basin Indians who lived on the edge of starvation were a constant irritant to overland travelers along the Humboldt River. Nothing seemed to discourage these natives from shooting livestock, horses, even dogs, with poisoned arrows in the hope the wounded animals would sicken and be left behind to be eaten.

Saturday August the 26th. Thursday we travailed eighteen miles. Friday morning one of my horses was missing, haveing got away through the night, and took the back track; and I with three others, went back about fifteen miles, following the road, and his tracks were fresh all of the way, but our animals that we rode being weary, and, not knowing how far the camp would move, we turned our course back, and comeing back, we saw a good many Indians. When we got to camp, I was somewhat tired, and they had travailed sixteen miles. The horse that I lost, was the one that I gave seventy dollars for. Today we met an imigration Company,[43] and there was one man with them belonging to the Church, from Salt Lake Vally, and he said that there was the best of grain there, and that corn grew fine, and all sorts of garden Sauce done well. And he calls it five hundred miles from here to Salt Lake settlement.[44] We travailed today twenty miles.

---

[43] The number of wagons, given by Henry Bigler as ten, suggests that this was the train guided by Peter Lassen, a forty-eight-year-old Danish promoter, who opened in 1848 a new branch of the trail to his ranch in the Sacramento Valley. If so, his followers would be lucky to survive the journey that year. Those who later took the circuitous northern route to the goldfields were to call it "Lassen's Horn," a sarcastic comparison to the trip by sea around the tip of South America. See *Bigler's Chronicle*, 122, and Devere and Helen Helfrich and Thomas Hunt, *Emigrant Trails West* (Klamath Falls, Oreg.: Trails West, Inc., 1984), ix.

[44] While Smith fails to identify the bearer of this information, the mileage estimate he gave indicates that he had come from Salt Lake Valley by way of Fort Hall on Snake River, near present Pocatello, Idaho, and suggests that he was another of the backsliders, like Hazen Kimball and Rogers, who had flown the new Mormon settlement. A possible clue to his identity is given in a letter on March 6, 1848, from church authorities at Salt Lake to Brigham Young which refers to a "Mr. Pollock" who had been "cut off the Church on the road" and left with Kimball and their families intending to "go to California." The only Utah pioneer of 1847 by this name was thirty-four-year-old James Pollock from Ireland who arrived at Salt Lake Valley with his wife, Priscilla, nineteen, and two children, Calrinda, six, and Thomas, two, in the first company of 100 under Daniel Spencer on September 24. See Letter from John Smith to Brigham Young, March 6, 1848, L.D.S. Journal History, quoted in Korns, "West from Fort Bridger," 261, and Carter, *Heart Throbs*, 8:419.

Tuesday August the 29th. Sunday we layed by; and Monday we travailed twenty two miles, and I caught a couple trout for supper, which went fine. Today I acompanied the wagons and this evening another train of wagons came in sight over the hills.[45]

Wednesday August the 30th. Today we travailed sixteen miles, being the most of the way throug[h] a canion.

Monday September the 4th. Last Thursday we travailed fifteen miles. Friday we travailed twenty miles. And Saturday we travailed ten miles, and in the evening we had [a] storm of rain and snow. Sunday we travailed twenty miles. Today we are laying by; and this morning while playing with one [of] the Boys, I fell on my shoulder, and hurt it pret[t]y bad, but ac[ci]dents will happen with the best of folks.

Tuesday Sept the 5th. Today we travailed five miles, when we encamped. I rode in a wagon [to]day, as my shoulder is very lame. We sent four men ahead, to find the turn off, to go across to Bear River, a cut off that the emigrants gave us a discription of.[46]

Wednesday Sept the [6th.] Today we travailed eighteen miles, when we came to the head of [the] Canion, where the Pilots left a paper for us to stop and encamp.

Thursday Sept the 7th. Today we travailed through the canion about twelve miles, when we encamped. The Pilots are here, and say

---

[45] Led by Joseph Ballinger Chiles, the forty-eight-wagon train met the eastbound Mormons near Gravelly Ford on the Humboldt River, about five miles east of present Beowawe, Nev. Although he had come by Fort Hall, the thirty-eight-year-old Kentuckian volunteered directions on a shortcut to Salt Lake Valley, possibly in part the route he had taken himself in 1841 as a member of the first overland party to California. Like Clyman and Cornwall, Chiles would take the new Carson trail, but add a refinement of his own to the route. Rather than go from the Humboldt Sink across the Forty-Mile-Desert to the Truckee River, he turned south at the sink, on the line of today's U.S. Highway 95, to meet the Carson River at a point, later known as Ragtown, seven miles west of present Fallon, Nev.

[46] This refers to the supposed Chiles shortcut to Salt Lake Valley.

Historic landmark on the California Trail is the Twin Sisters at the junction of the Salt Lake Cutoff and Fort Hall road in the Silent City of Rocks, near present Almo, Idaho.

that they did not see any place, that they thought a prop[er] place for turning across for Bear River.

Friday Sept the 8th. Last night at a me[e]ting, to decide which way to go, there was some disputeing, but finally we concluded to take Mr. Childs,es cut o[ff][47] Acordingly today we went up on the hill, about eight miles, [sending] the Pilots ahead to find water, and if they found water they [were] to raise a smoke, for us to come to[o] and just at night s[ome] of them came back not finding any water, but Brother S[ly] and Diamond went another way, and have not got back.

Saturday Sept. the 9th. 48 Last evening brother Sly and Diamond came back haveing found water, but at a me[e]ting this morning, the camp concluded to go back and take the other cut off,[48] and hitched up and went back to the old camp ground and encamped there.

Sunday Sept. the 10th. Today we travailed fifteen miles, and have now left Marys River.

Monday September the 11th. Today we travailed fourteen miles when we met the pilot comeing back; and he said that he had been ahead four miles to another watering place but there was no feed, So they came back to encamp where there was feed; and the most of the wagons had got ahead some ways and had to come back.

Tuesday Sept. the 12th. 48 We travailed 17 miles and encamped on Goose Creek.[49]

----

[47] At the head of the Humboldt, some ten miles north of present Wells, Nev., the camp debated whether to keep looking for the route Chiles had described or stay on the road toward Fort Hall and take a later shortcut. Since Chiles had been mistaken or misunderstood, their decision would cost two day's travel.

[48] Unreported by Smith, the Mormons had learned about this shortcut on August 27 from Samuel J. Hensley who had discovered it only a few days before while traveling west with a small pack party. A California pioneer of 1843, the Kentuckian was thirty-two when he opened the important route, known as the Salt Lake Cutoff. See *Bigler's Chronicle*, 123.

[49] Following the Fort Hall road, the company crossed the line of to-day's U.S. Highway 93 fourteen miles north of Wells, Nev., and moved up Thousand Springs Valley to cross the rim of the Great Basin to Goose Creek which flows northward across the northwest corner of Utah to enter the Snake River at Burley, Idaho. See *Emigrant Trails West*, 39.

Wednesday September the 13th. We travailed sixteen miles down Goose Creek, in which this evening there was a great many small trout caught.

Thursday Sept. the 14th. This morning the Pilots went ahead, to find the cut off; and we travailed seven miles down the Creek, and then left it and travailed three miles, when we came to a Spring, where we were to stop, till the Pilots came; and we stop[p]ed there two or three hours, when Brother Thompson came, and said that there was a place about four miles ahead, that would do the camp. So we hitched up and started, but haveing some very bad hills to come up, we did not get encamped till just dark.[50] Brother Sly came after a little haveing found the turn off place.

Friday Sept. the 15th. Today we travailed seven miles, then left the old road,[51] and travailed two miles farther and encamped on Cajvese (Casver,) a french name.[52]

Saturday Sept. the 16th. We travailed ten miles in an easterly direction, and encamped again on Cajvese, in a notch of the mountains. We saw several Indians on horseback.

Sunday Sept. the 17th. We travailed ten miles farther, in easterly direction, and encamped by a Spring,[53] at the point of a Mountain.

---

[50] Having left Goose Creek, they camped near Granite Pass in the Goose Creek Mountains on the present Idaho-Utah border.

[51] The junction of the Fort Hall road and Hensley's Salt Lake Cutoff is overlooked by the Twin Sisters, two towering rock formations in the Silent City of Rocks, near present Almo, Idaho. The landmark, one of the most distinctive on the California Trail, was named by Addison Pratt of Smith's company which became the first to take wagons over the new cutoff. See *Bigler's Chronicle*, 127.

[52] This apparently refers to *Cajeux*, "little raft," the early French-American name for the upper stretch of Raft River, a tributary of the Snake River.

[53] This camp was on Clear Creek, near present Naf, Idaho, on the Idaho-Utah border. For more detailed information, see Korns, "West from Fort Bridger" and L. A. Fleming and A. R. Standing, "The Salt Lake Cutoff," *Utah Historical Quarterly* 33 (1965): 248–71.

Monday Sept. the 18th. Today we travailed eleven miles through a pass of the Mountains, and encamped on the side of a Mountain, in sight of Salt Lake.

Tuesday Sept. the 19th. Today we travailed fifteen miles across a plain and encamped on deep Creek,[54] haveing been named that by Mr. Hensly as where he crossed it, it was so deep that he had to make a bridge.

Wednesday September the 20th. Today we travailed five miles up the creek, and then left it, and travailed ten miles farther and encamped by a Spring in the Mountains.[55]

Friday Sept. the 22nd. 48 Yesterday we travailed fourteen miles and encamped on the head of a Stream of poor water.[56]
Today we travailed twenty three miles, and encamped on a small Stream about a mile from Bear river,[57] where we caught plenty of fish.

Saturday Sept. the 23d. 48 We crossed the stream which was very bad, and one wagon got broke, but we fixed it up and travailed about

----

[54] The Deep Creek camp was located about six miles west of present Snowville, Utah, on State Route 30.

[55] Hansel Spring Valley, where the company camped about five miles southeast of Snowville, and the nearby Hansel Mountains are the closest any Utah geographical feature comes to preserving the name of Samuel Hensley for his contributions to overland travel. A leader in the California conquest and known as "generous, temperate, and brave," the discoverer of the Salt Lake Cutoff died at Warm Springs, Calif., at age forty-nine. See Bancroft, *History of California*, 3:781.

[56] Blue Springs, located about three miles north of present Howell, Utah, on Interstate 84, provided the most brackish water on the cutoff.

[57] About three miles south of present Tremonton, the company camped on the west bank of Malad River which got its name from French trappers who became sick after eating the flesh of beavers caught along the waterway. The stream is a tributary of Bear River which empties into the Great Salt Lake. See Warren A. Ferris, *Life in the Rocky Mountains*, Paul C. Phillips, ed. (Denver: Old West Publishing Company, 1940), 66–67.

four miles and encamped. There are old wagon tracks here that lead to Salt Lake Settlements.[58]

1848. Sunday Sept. the 24th. We travailed eighteen miles down Bear Vally.[59]

Monday Sept. the 25th. We travailed twenty miles and encamped by Captain Browns,[60] and bought some cheese.

Tuesday Sept. the 26th. Today we bought some mellons, grean cor[n] &c. as we are laying by, for yesterday the cannons was left back about ten miles, and today we sent back and brought them up.

---

[58] Then as today, the stream was "narrow, not very deep," according to Bigler, but the bottom was "soft and muddy" to make the ford hazardous. After crossing, the company went on to ford Bear River, near Honeyville, Utah, and camp on the east bank where they saw wagon tracks, probably made earlier that year by Hazen Kimball and other disaffected Mormons on their way to Fort Hall.

[59] This distance would place the company in the vicinity of present Brigham City, Utah.

[60] He was the same Captain James Brown who had commanded a detachment to Pueblo in 1846 and met battalion veterans from California near Donner Lake a year later on his way to Monterey to claim the mustering out pay of Pueblo battalion members which came to about $5,000, mostly in gold. On his return, Brown at the direction of the church governing council at Salt Lake spent $1,950 of the battalion money he had collected to buy the rights of Miles Goodyear to the trading post, Fort Buenaventura, near the confluence of the Ogden and Weber rivers. Known as Brownsville at the time of Smith's arrival, the little settlement became Ogden City in 1850. Years later, when Mormon forms of communal land ownership were being challenged, some family members claimed that Brown had received $10,000 in Spanish doubloons to pay off the Pueblo veterans and purchased Goodyear's claims with his own share of this money and other funds at a price of $3,000, but early records disprove this. For the correct story, see B. H. Roberts, *The Mormon Battalion, Its History and Achievements* (Salt Lake City: Deseret News, 1919), 61–63, and Dale L. Morgan, "Miles Goodyear and the Founding of Ogden," *Utah Historical Quarterly* 21 (1953): 317–19. For the variant version, see Edward W. Tullidge, *Tullidge's Histories, Vol. II, History of Northern Utah and Southern Idaho* (Salt Lake City: From the Press of the Juvenile Instructor, 1889), 1–14. The founder of Ogden died of an accident in 1863 at age sixty-two.

Wednesday September the 27th. We left the most of the Cavia[61] to be herded, and I took my horse, but left my Mule and Ma[re] with the herd. After travailing eighteen miles we encamped.[62]

Thursday Sept. the 28th. I rode ahead and about two oclo[ck] arived at Salt Lake City; and after riding about considerable found Father, Mother, Sisters and brother; and they were all w[ell].[63] They were liveing four miles from the city, on the place where [he] put in his crop, such as Wheat, Corn, Peas, Beans and other gar[den] Sauce, but the crickets ate up or spoiled the most of it. But [he] has saved twelve bushel of Wheat, and has got some corn, Bea[ns], Peas, Mellons &c. growing.

Friday Sept. the 29th. Today I took my Horse, and went with Father and Candace down to t[he] City, to get my Clothing;[64] and with some trouble I found it and pack[ed] [it] home; and Mr. Diamond came up with us; and we gave him as ma[ny] Mellons &c. as he could eat.

---

[61] Another variation of the Spanish word, *caballada*, for drove of horses.

[62] From just south of Ogden, the early road ran between today's Interstate 15 and the shore of the Great Salt Lake near the present towns of Hooper and Syracuse.

[63] After more than two years, Azariah Smith, now twenty, was at last reunited with his mother, Esther Dutcher Smith, thirty-seven, two sisters, Emily, sixteen, and Candace, fourteen, and younger brother, Joseph, just turned four, who had arrived in Salt Lake Valley themselves only days before. Before winter, the family would move into a two-room adobe house, built by Albert Smith on the southeastern outskirts of the new city, probably in or near the present suburb of Sugarhouse.

[64] From the more than $500 in gold he brought back from California, he also "went to Pres. Brigham Young, and paid my tithing, also donating Some for the poor and one dollar each to the twelve," Smith said in his autobiography, written in his own hand years later. See manuscript, "Biography of Albert and Azariah Smith," donated by the editor on July 19, 1988, to the California State Library, California Section, Sacramento.

EPILOGUE

After traveling by foot, horseback, and wagon more than 3,000 miles in twenty-six months, Azariah Smith was at last home and ready to stay there for good. Not for fifty years, except for short trips to attend church conferences at Salt Lake City, would he venture far enough from Manti, Utah, where he settled in 1849, to be away from home two nights in a row.

Then, early in 1898, he and his three comrades from Sutter's Mill received engraved invitations, round-trip tickets on the railroad, and $20 each for expenses to come to San Francisco for the Golden Jubilee of the gold discovery, a half century before. The youngest at sixty-nine, Smith traveled with William J. Johnston, then seventy-three, to the depot at Ogden, Utah, where they met eighty-three-year-old Henry W. Bigler, who had ridden the stage from his home at St. George 130 miles to the nearest railroad station at Milford, Utah, and James S. Brown, also sixty-nine.

On January 22, the four surviving eyewitnesses of Marshall's historic discovery arrived at San Francisco where they were met by John H. Jewett, president of the Society of California Pioneers; John S. Hittell, San Francisco journalist-historian; and society officials, Almarin B. Paul and General W. H. Pratt, and escorted to their rooms at the Russ House. The *San Francisco Chronicle* noted that Bigler suffered from a severe cold and described Smith as one who "considers himself quite a young man still, though his hair is white with the frost of nearly 70 years."[1]

The Jubilee Parade on the fiftieth anniversary, January 24, 1898, was the most spectacular event San Francisco would witness, short of the great earthquake and fire, eight years later. Up to 14,000

---

[1] Golden Jubilee Edition, *Sunday Chronicle*, San Francisco, January 23, 1898, 30.

The Golden Jubilee parade on the fiftieth anniversary of the California gold discovery was the most spectacular event San Francisco would see short of the great earthquake and fire eight years later. Front page, *San Francisco Chronicle*, January 24, 1898.

marched or rode in the procession, 837 on horses and more than 1,400 in carriages or floats drawn by some 700 splendidly groomed animals. Nearly 600 musicians played in the thirty bands that marched that day. For the grand procession to pass the Chronicle Building took two hours and twenty-five minutes. At the center of all the excitement, Smith described the day's events in his journal:[2]

---

[2] Quotes on the Golden Jubilee of the gold discovery are from Azariah Smith's regular journal during the period from January 20 to February 5, 1898.

"I put on a white shirt, and Mr. Hittell came, wishing us to be ready soon for the Coach, and soon it came, and we were helped into it by an officer of the day.

"And on each Side of the coach, were placed in large letters, THE COMPANIONS OF MARSHALL, and we were introduced to many of the officers, and notable men of the City. And at 10 oc 40 *min* we were formed in the Procession, and Bro. Johnston was given an American Flag, one side of the Coach, and me, the Cal. Pioneers Flag with a large Bear painted on it, on the other side. And the Procession made a grand show, with many nice Floats, wagons, coaches &c. also soldiers, with music, and Boys, and Girls, and Ladies, &c., extending a long distance down the street, being verry full of Spectators on either side, also the windows being full, and waving Hankerchiefs &c. with ap[p]lause. And after marching some distance, in good order, they were Counter marched, back with much Aplause, many greeting us on the way. The streets were well lighted, and decorated, making a grand sight indeed.

"Bro. Bigler, feeling poorly, was taken to his room at the Hotel. And some officers came, and had us taken to the large Pavilion and leading us through the Croud, up on to the stand, by the side of the pulpit, where there was reserved seats for us. The room, and also the Gal[l]ery, was well filled with Spectators, being beautifully adorned for the ocasion.

"Many of the officers, again shaking hands with us, with respect and good wishes. Opening by singing, and Prayer, and some songs, recitations, &c. also a long speech. And then one speaking of the Gold Discovery by Marshall in 1848 being the main stay and impetus for the building up of Cal[ifornia]. And a speaker then speaking of the four Companions of Marshall, now living, and with them on the Stand, and wishing to introduce us to the as[s]embly, and as our names were called to Arise.

"And my name being called first, I arose and Speaking Somewhat of my former life, and being one of the members of the Mormon Bat[talion] and also at the building of Sutter's Saw mill at the finding of the first Gold, in Cal. and introducing me to the large Asembly, amid much ap[p]laus[e], and then, the other three names were also called, and introduced to the Asembly, Speaking of us in high terms, and then three Cheers, were given for the Companions of Marshall, which was hearty indeed.

"And in the evening, I and Johnston, went with a guide to a Beautiful Dancing room, Seeing some good dancing, mostly waltzing. We were waited upon well, and given some ice cream. And being introduced to many Gentlemen, and Ladies."

For a full week, the old battalion comrades posed for photographs, answered questions, shook countless hands, visited the shipyards, and attended special events in their honor. They went to the San Francisco Zoo where they saw "the largest Bear, under controll in the world," and toured the "most notable Buildings in the City" with "some of the most Beautiful rooms, and Scenery that I ever beheld."

Also during this time, the Society of California Pioneers apparently took advantage of the opportunity to resolve two controversies over the gold discovery that continue to this day. On January 28, Smith recorded, "Prest. Jewitt came with my [train] ticket extended for another month. And wishing us to Sign a Certificate, Certifying, that we were with Marshall at the first discovery of Gold." Two days later, at a reception of society officials and wives, he wrote:

"Mr. Jewitt, the executive of the Comittee, in a kind and jovial way, speaking to each of us, and put[t]ing a present of money in our hand, And it being their wish, we signed 8 or 10 autographs for them. And they also gave us each a book with a Photo of us, and also many of the Pioneer Soci[e]ty in it. Also a scetch of the finding of the first Gold in Cal. and many nice pictures in it. And Mr. Jewitt spoke some time, verry truthfully and highly of us. And by request, we signed a paper, Certifying that the first Gold was found on the 24*th* of Jan,y 1848."

The first document the four men signed apparently attempted to dispel doubt that Johnston was actually at the mill on the day of the discovery as he claimed. The other undoubtedly sought to correct Marshall's recollection, made years after the event, that the date of his historic find was January 19, five days earlier. The location of both documents, if they survived the 1906 earthquake and fire, is unknown.

Two of the Mormon visitors, Brown and Johnston, elected to stay longer in San Francisco, but Azariah Smith by January 31 was ready, as always, to go home. He boarded the train that day with Bigler, still suffering from a severe cold, and went back to Utah to report on the jubilee to leaders of his faith before returning to Manti where he found "my Wife well, and glad to see me home again."

After that trip, he dedicated himself entirely to church work at the Mormon temple in his community, completed in 1888, which he visited often enough from his nearby house to cover by his calculation some 7,000 miles, just going back and forth over a span of nearly twenty-five years.

As a child, Hazel Anderson Bigler remembered him in 1910 as a slender, gentle man with a pink nose and a white beard that reached to his waist who came to her house every afternoon for a meal of "garden sauce" and a nap. Unlike Henry Bigler, a lifelong missionary, Smith never bore his testimony at church, she remembered, or had much to say at any other time. "There was no preach in him, but he always wrote a great deal," she said.

Azariah Smith kept his journal up to date until his last year, 1912, when he passed away quietly in September at the age of eighty-four and was buried in the Manti Cemetery where he lies with the rest of his pioneer family in the place he always wanted to be—home.

INDEX

153

Fages, Pedro, 93
First Missouri Mounted Volunteers, 6-7, 11, 13
Fort Buenaventura, 145n.60
Fort Churchill, 135 (ill.), 136n.35
Fort Churchill Road, 136n.35
Fort Hall, 121, 145n.58
Fort Hall road, 141 (ill.), 142nn.47&49, 143n.51
Fort Leavenworth, 7, 11, 13-14, 18, 86n.35
Fort Moore Hill, 86n.34
Fort Pueblo, 27n.43, 39, 47, 48
Fort Stockton, *See* Presidio Hill
Forty-Mile Desert, 136n.37, 137n.39
Foster, Stephen, 40, 48n.26, 57
Foster's Hole, New Mexico, 48n.26
Frémont, John C., 38, 39, 70, 71, 74n.11, 79n, 86n.35, 96n.9, 98nn.14&16, 132n.27
Gadsden Purchase, 41
Gale, William A., 81n.26
Galisteo Creek, 43n.10
Galland, Isaac, 15n.8
Garcés, Fancisco Tomás Hermenegildo, 59n.49, 96n.9
Genoa, Nevada, 134n.32
Geothermal Food Processors, 137n.38
Gila [Ahelia] River, 40, 41, 48n.26, 59n.49, 60, 61, 63, 64
Gila Trail, 42 (ill.)
Gold rush. *See* California gold rush
Goodyear, Miles, 145n.60
Goose Creek, 142-43
Goose Creek Mountains, 143n.50
Grande River. *See* Rio Grande
Grant, Jedediah M., 137n.40
Gravelly Ford, Humboldt River, 140n.45
Gravelly Ford, San Joaquin River, 98n.16
Great Basin 97n.13, 142n.48
Great Basin Indians ("Diggers"), 138n.42
Great Britain, territorial designs on Pacific Coast, 2-3, 5, 9
Great Central Valley (California), 96n.8
Great Salt Lake, 93, 100, 111, 112, 117, 144

Great Salt Lake Valley, 91, 99n.19, 102, 111n.47, 113, 116, 118, 122, 125, 129n.20, 137n.40, 139
Green River, 100nn.19&21
Guadalupe Mountains, 52n.33, 52-53
Guadalupe Pass, 52n.33
Gudde, Erwin G., vii

Half-Breed Tract, 15n.8
Hall, Mike, 49n.26
Hammond, Francis, 127n.16
Hampton, James, 46-47
Hancock, Levi, 76, 87n.37, 88, 93
Hanks, Ephraim, 49-50
Hansel Mountains, 144n.55
Hansel Spring Valley, 144n.55
Harlan-Young Party, 105n
Hastings Cutoff, 105n
Hawkins, Benjamin, 116n.59
Hensley, Samual J., 142n.48, 143n.51, 144
Higgins, Nelson, 27n.43, 46
Hittell, John S., 147, 149
Holmes, Jonathan H., 116
Hope Valley, 133
Howells, T. C. D., 88n.43
Hudson, Wilford, 113n.51, 115, 129n.21, 130, 131
Humboldt River, 124, 136n.37, 137n.39, 138n.42, 140n.45, 142n.47
Hunt, Jefferson, 21n.27, 22, 23n.33, 89n.46, 93, 100, 111n.47
Hunt, Thomas H., 123n
Hunter, Jesse D., 86n.36, 87n.38, 88n.41
Hunter, Lydia, 25n.38, 82
Hyde, William, 87n.38, 88n.43, 93

Illinois, 9, 13, 15
Iowa, 4, 7, 8, 9, 11, 15
Isletta [Lolettah], New Mexico, 44
Ivie, Richard, 87n.40

Jackson, Andrew, 1
Janos, Mexico, 50nn.29&30
Jewett, John H., 147, 150
Johnson, —, 83
Johnson, William, 101n.23
Johnson's Ranch, 101n.24, 103